SMOKER COOKBOOK

The Art of Smoking Meat for the Best Barbecue Ever

ROGER MURPHY

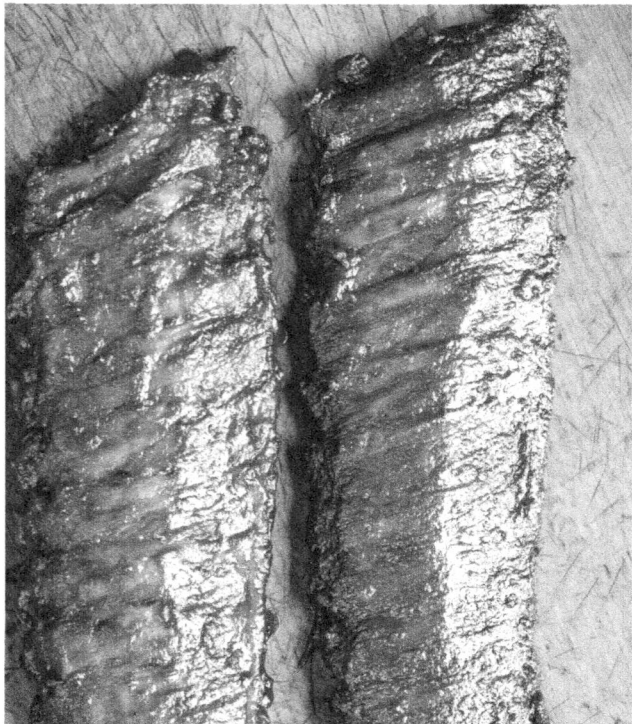

CONTENTS

Chapter 1: BEEF..8
Chapter 2: PORK..28
Chapter 3: LAMB..47
Chapter 4: CHICKEN...64
Chapter 5: TURKEY..82
Chapter 6: FISH AND SEAFOOD..........................94
Chapter 7: BURGERS, SAUSAGES, AND MORE......126
Chapter 8: GAME MEATS...................................146
Chapter 9: VEGGIES..170
Chapter 10: SAUCES..182
Chapter 11: SMOKING MEAT BASICS...................196
Chapter 12: SAFETY..209

INTRODUCTION

With clear and concise instructions, this book shows you how to get the most out of your smoker. This book provides detailed instructions on how to smoke meats, seafood, game, and vegetables, as well as tips on selecting the best cuts of meat and choosing the correct wood chips for flavor. Although the cookbook contains irresistible recipes guaranteed to please, including classic favorites like pulled pork and beef brisket, you'll also find exciting dishes like smoked chicken wings, tuna fillets, and even cold-smoked duck breast. Are you looking for a delicious way to add extra flavor to your meals? The sauces chapter is perfect for spicing up your dishes. Are you looking to perfect your smoked meat game? With beautiful photos and easy-to-follow steps, this book will help you take your smoking to the next level. Look no further than this fantastic smoker cookbook with everything you need to know about smoking meat, including how to choose the right smoker, what cuts of meat work best, and how to create flavorful recipes that impress you, your friends, and your family. Whether you're a beginner or a seasoned pro, this cookbook is a must-have for any smoker's library!

WHY SMOKING

Smoking is generally used as one of the cooking methods nowadays. With modern cooking techniques, food enriched in protein, such as meat, would spoil if cooked for extended periods. Whereas, Smoking is a low & slow process of cooking meat. Where there is smoke, there is a flavor. With white smoke, you can boost the taste of your food. In addition to this statement, you can also preserve the nutrition in the food. Smoking is flexible & one of the oldest techniques of making food. You must brush the marinade over your food while you cook and let the miracle happen. The only thing you need to do is to add a handful of fresh wood chips when required. Just taste your regular grilled and smoked meat, and you will find the difference. Remember one thing, i.e., "Smoking is an art." With a bit of time & practice, even you can become an expert. Once you become an expert in smoking techniques, you will never look for other cooking techniques. To find which smoking technique works for you, you must experiment with different woods & cooking methods. Just cook the meat over an indirect heat source & cook it for hours. When smoking your meats, you must let the smoke escape & move around.

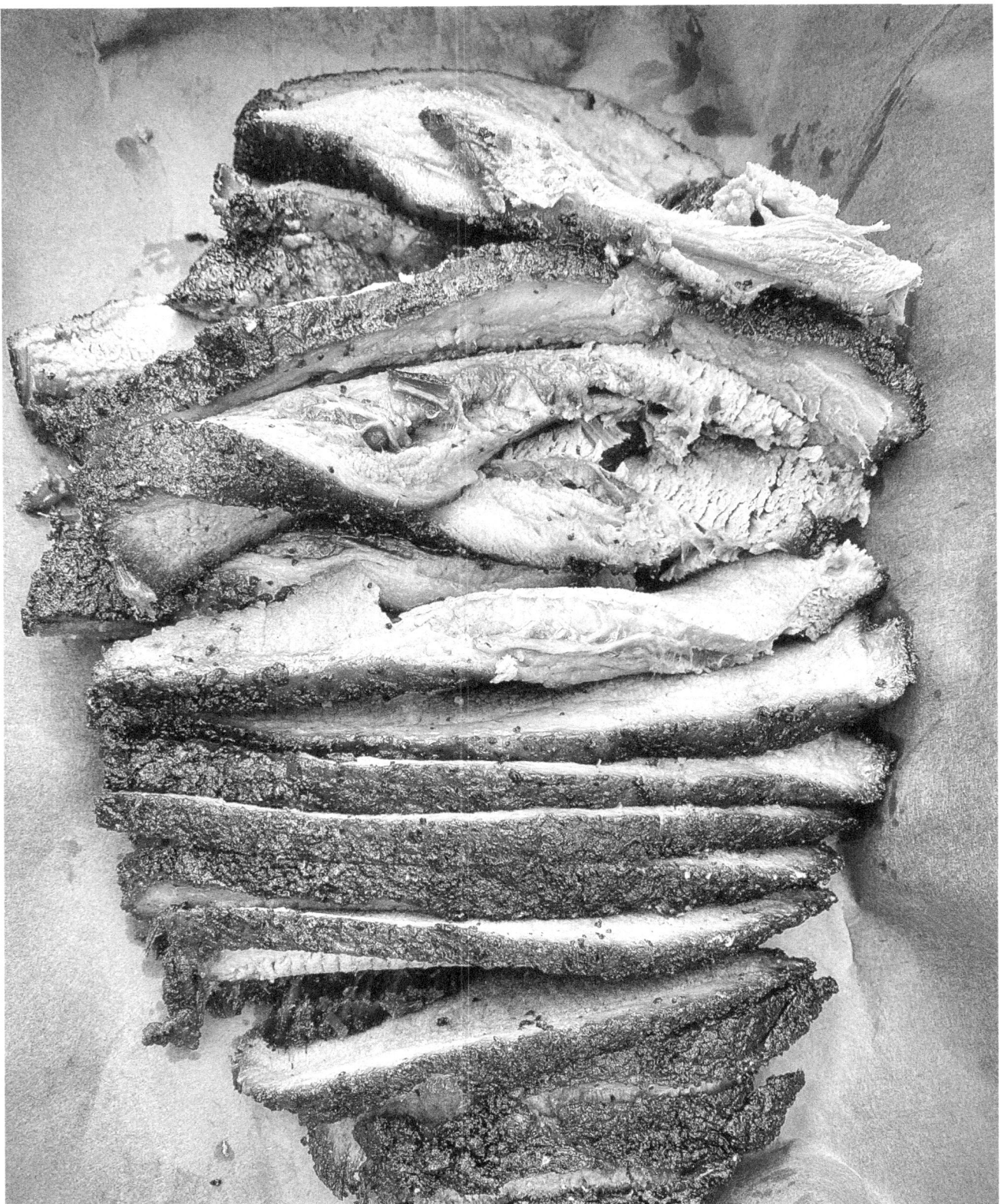

CHAPTER 1
BEEF

SMOKED BEEF RIBS - 11

SMOKED BRISKET - 13

TUSCAN-STYLE SHORT BEEF RIBS WITH PASTA IN TOMATO SAUCE - 15

HICKORY SMOKED WHISKEY MEATLOAF - 17

SHREDDED BEEF TACOS - 19

TEXAS-RUBBED BEEF BRISKET - 21

OAK SMOKED TRI-TIP STEAK - 24

ARTICHOKE AND SPINACH SMOKED FATTY - 26

SMOKED BEEF RIBS

(TOTAL COOK TIME 9 HOURS 15 MINUTES)

INGREDIENTS FOR 4 SERVINGS

THE MEAT

- 1 4-bone section beef ribs (4-lb, 1.8-kg)

THE INGREDIENTS

- Horseradish flavor Dijon mustard, any brand – 2 tablespoons
- Beef rub, any brand – 6 tablespoons

THE SPRITZ

- Hot sauce, any brand – ¼ cup
- White vinegar - 1 cup'

THE SMOKE

- Set the smoker to 250°F (120°C) for indirect cooking
- Hickory or oak wood chips work well for this recipe

METHOD

1. Cover the beef ribs with the flavored mustard, and season generously all over with beef rub.
2. Transfer the ribs to the preheated smoker, and insert a meat thermometer, programmed to 200°F (90°C) in the thickest part of the ribs while not touching the bone. Close the smoker's lid and smoke the ribs for 3 hours.
3. Add the hot sauce and white vinegar to a spray bottle and shake to combine.
4. Once the ribs have smoked for 3 hours, start to spritz them every 40-60 minutes. Continue to smoke until they register an internal temperature of 200°F (90°C). The whole smoking process will take approximately 8-10 hours.
5. Take the beef ribs out of the smoker and wrap them in aluminum foil. Set aside to rest in an insulated cooler for a minimum of 60 minutes before slicing.
6. Enjoy.

SMOKED BRISKET

(TOTAL COOK TIME 19 HOURS 35 MINUTES)

INGREDIENTS FOR 12 SERVINGS

THE MEAT

- Beef brisket, excess fat trimmed (11-lb, 5-kg)
- Apple cider vinegar, as needed, to spritz

THE RUB

- Coarse salt, divided – 3 tablespoons + ¼ cup
- Mustard or olive oil – 3-4 tablespoons
- Coarse black pepper – ½ cup
- Paprika – ¼ cup
- Garlic powder – 2 tablespoons

THE SMOKE

- Set the smoker to 225°F (105°C)

METHOD

1. Season the beef brisket with 3 tablespoons of salt and place it on a cooling rack. Transfer the meat, uncovered, to the fridge, for 8-12 hours.
2. The following day, spread the mustard or olive oil all over the brisket, rubbing it in well.
3. Mix the black pepper with the remaining coarse salt, paprika, and garlic powder in a bowl, and whisk well. Tip the mixture over the brisket and rub it all over to cover fully.
4. Add some apple cider vinegar to a spray bottle.
5. Smoke the brisket for 4-6 hours or until it registers an internal temperature of 165°F (75°C). You will need to spritz the meat with the apple cider vinegar every 60 minutes. When the brisket is at the desired internal temperature, remove it from the smoker and wrap in aluminum foil. Return to the smoker and smoke for another 4-6 hours or until the meat registers 205°F (95°C).
6. Remove the meat from the smoker and allow to rest for 10-120 minutes.
7. Slice the brisket against the grain and serve.

TUSCAN-STYLE SHORT BEEF RIBS WITH PASTA IN TOMATO SAUCE

(TOTAL COOK TIME 7 HOURS)

INGREDIENTS FOR 2 SERVINGS

THE MEAT

- Beef short ribs (2-lb, 0.9-kg)

THE INGREDIENTS

- Olive oil – 1 tablespoon
- Kosher salt, divided – 1½ teaspoons
- Black pepper, divided – 1½ teaspoons
- Apple cider vinegar, for spritzing

THE PASTA AND SAUCE

- Pappardelle pasta (8-oz, 200-gm)
- Extra-virgin olive oil – 2 tablespoons
- Mushrooms (4-oz, 110-gm)
- Black pepper – ⅛ teaspoon
- Salt, as needed
- 2-3 garlic cloves, peeled
- 1 can tomato sauce, reduced to 2 cups (28-oz, 800-gm)
- Parmesan cheese, freshly grated – ¼ cup
- Pecorino cheese, freshly grated – ¼ cup
- Fresh Italian parsley – 2 tablespoons

THE SMOKE

- Set the smoker to 275°F (135°C)

METHOD

1. Add the ribs to a big bowl, along with 1 tablespoon of olive oil, to bind. Then season with 1½ teaspoons of salt and 1½ teaspoons of black pepper. Place the short ribs on the smoker grill. Around every 40-45 minutes, spritz the ribs with apple cider vinegar. Cook the ribs for about 5½ hours or until the meat registers an internal temperature of no less than 185°F (85°C). Remove the ribs from the smoker and allow them to cool while you prepare the pasta.
2. Cook the pasta according to the package instructions and until al dente.
3. For the sauce, heat a skillet and add 2 tablespoons of oil. Then add the mushrooms along with ⅛ teaspoon of black pepper and a pinch of salt. Cook for approximately 5 minutes until the mushrooms sweat and expel their moisture. Next, add the garlic and the meat, followed by the tomato sauce. You may want to add a splash of pasta cooking water to thin out the consistency of the sauce. Add both of the cheeses and parsley and stir to combine.
4. Add the drained pasta to a platter, and spoon over the sauce.
5. Serve with the ribs, and enjoy.

HICKORY SMOKED WHISKEY MEATLOAF

(TOTAL COOK TIME 4 HOURS 15 MINUTES)

INGREDIENTS FOR 6 SERVINGS

THE MEAT

- Ground beef (2-lb, 0.9-kg)

THE INGREDIENTS

- Panko breadcrumbs – ½ cup
- ½ medium red onion, peeled and grated
- 2 garlic cloves, peeled and minced
- 2 eggs, lightly beaten
- Worcestershire sauce – 1 tablespoon
- Jack Daniels whiskey – 2 tablespoons
- Steak rub – 1 tablespoon
- Milk – ¼ cup
- Pepper Jack cheese, cut into strips (6-oz, 150-gm)

THE SAUCE

- Ketchup – ½ cup
- Brown sugar - ⅓ cup
- Jack Daniels whiskey – ¼ cup
- Steak rub – 1 tablespoon
- Crushed red pepper flakes – 2 teaspoons

THE SMOKE

- Set the smoker to 225°F (105°C) for indirect smoking
- Hickory wood chips work well for this recipe

METHOD

1. In a big bowl, combine the beef with the breadcrumbs, onion, garlic, eggs, Worcestershire sauce, whiskey, steak rub, and milk. Using clean hands, gently mix until combined.
2. Spread around half of the meat mixture on the bottom of a grill basket. Next, layer on the cheese, allowing a space of around 1-in (2-cm) of meatloaf on all sides. Then top with the remaining meat mixture and press the edges together to seal in the cheese while smoking.
3. Mix the sauce ingredients (ketchup, sugar, whiskey, steak rub, and red pepper flakes) in a smaller bowl.
4. Place the meatloaf on the smoker and cook until its internal temperature registers 165°F (75°C), for approximately 4 hours.
5. Remove from the smoker and allow to rest for 3-4 minutes before slicing.
6. Enjoy.

SHREDDED BEEF TACOS

(TOTAL COOK TIME 6 HOURS 15 MINUTES)

INGREDIENTS FOR 8 SERVINGS

THE MEAT

- Beef chuck roast (3-lb, 1.5-kg)

THE INGREDIENTS

- Chipotle garlic rub, store-bought, any brand – 4 tablespoons
- 1 bottle beer
- 1 jar hatch chilies (16-oz, 500-gm)
- 1 can jalapeno salsa (8-oz, 200-gm)
- 8 corn tortillas
- Toppings of choice, as needed

THE SMOKE

- Set the smoker to 200°F (90°C) for indirect smoking

METHOD

1. Cover the meat all over with the chipotle garlic rub.
2. Place the meat on the smoker and roast for 3-4 hours.
3. Place the beef roast in a Dutch oven. Pour the beer of the meat and spoon over the hatch chilies and salsa. Braise on the grill, in the oven, or on the stovetop for 3-4 hours until the meat is easy to shred and fork-tender.
4. Shred the meat.
5. In a skillet, heat the tortillas along with a drop of oil. Stuff with the shredded beef and top with your favorite topping.
6. Enjoy.

TEXAS-RUBBED BEEF BRISKET

(TOTAL COOK TIME 19 HOURS 20 MINUTES)

INGREDIENTS FOR 8 SERVINGS

THE MEAT

- Beef brisket, untrimmed (8-lbs, 4-kgs)

THE RUB

- Ancho chili powder- 3 tablespoons
- Sea salt – 2 tablespoons
- Ground allspice – 1 tablespoon
- Celery seeds – 1 tablespoon
- Garlic powder – 1 tablespoon
- Ground coriander seeds – 1 tablespoon
- Ground mustard seeds – 1 tablespoon
- Hungarian smoked paprika – 1 tablespoon
- Dried oregano – 1 tablespoon
- Freshly ground black pepper – 1 tablespoon
- Fresh apple juice– 2 cups
- Texas BBQ sauce, store-bought, of choice, warmed, as needed

THE SMOKE

- Before cooking, pre-soak 3 cups of pecan wood chips in water for 2-3 hours
- Preheat smoker to 225°F (110°C) using hardwood charcoal and the soaked wood chips.

METHOD

1. First, prepare the rub. In a bowl, combine the Ancho chili powder, sea salt, allspice, celery seeds, garlic powder, coriander seeds, mustard seeds, smoked paprika, oregano, and black pepper.
2. Rub the spice mix over the beef brisket, cover tightly with kitchen wrap, and transfer to the fridge to chill overnight.
3. Around 60 minutes before you start to cook, allow the beef brisket to come to room temperature.
4. Place the brisket on the smoker grate fat side facing upwards and close the smoker lid.
5. Add the apple juice to a spray bottle.
6. Spray the meat with apple juice every 2 hours. Doing this will help to keep it moist.
7. After around 4 hours, or when the internal temperature of the beef registers 165°F (75°C), wrap the brisket in aluminum foil and cook for an additional 4 hours.
8. When the beef registers an internal temperature of 185°F (85°C), remove from the smoker and set aside for 15-20 minutes before slicing.
9. Serve the beef brisket with your choice of warmed Texas BBQ sauce and enjoy.

OAK SMOKED TRI-TIP STEAK

(TOTAL COOK TIME 2 HOURS)

INGREDIENTS FOR 8 SERVINGS

THE MEAT

- Tri-tip steak beef, patted dry (3-lbs, 1.4-kgs)

THE INGREDIENTS

- Kosher salt – 3 tablespoons
- Freshly ground black pepper – 3 tablespoons

THE SMOKE

- Preheat, the smoker to 225- 250°F (110-120°C)
- Use oak wood chips for this recipe

METHOD

1. Rub the meat all over with salt and pepper.
2. Smoke for 60-90 minutes until the meat registers an internal temperature of 130°F (55°C).
3. Remove the meat from the smoker and wrap tightly in parchment paper. Return the meat to the smoker and cook for an additional 30-60 minutes until it registers at an internal temperature of 135-140°F (55-60°C).
4. Remove the meat from the smoker and set aside for 20 minutes before slicing against the grain.
5. Serve and enjoy.

ARTICHOKE AND SPINACH SMOKED FATTY

(TOTAL COOK TIME 2 HOURS 10 MINUTES)

INGREDIENTS FOR 8 SERVINGS

THE MEAT

- Ground beef (2-lbs, 0.9-kgs)
- Bacon rashers (2-lbs, 0.9-kgs)

THE FILLING

- Parmesan cheese, shredded (4-ozs, 113-gms)
- Ricotta cheese (1-lb, 0.45-kgs)
- Canned artichoke hearts, chopped (8-ozs, 225-gms)
- 2 garlic cloves, peeled and crushed
- Zest and juice of 1 lemon
- Beef seasoning – 2 tablespoons
- Frozen, chopped spinach, thawed and drained (6-ozs, 170-gms)
- Kosher salt – 2 teaspoons

THE SMOKE

- After resting, when ready to cook, preheat your smoker to 250°F (120°C)
- We recommend hickory or oak wood for this recipe

METHOD

1. First, prepare the filling. Combine the Parmesan, ricotta, artichoke, garlic, lemon zest, lemon juice, beef seasoning, spinach, and 1 teaspoon salt in a bowl using clean hands. Set to one side.
2. Arrange a sheet of plastic wrap on your worktop. Take one bacon rasher and place it on the plastic wrap vertically. Arrange pieces of bacon horizontally, alternating each horizontal strip so that one is under the vertical strip, and the next is on top. Keep going until you have a square piece of weaved bacon.
3. Place the ground beef on top of the bacon weave and gently press it down into an even layer. Make sure to leave a border of bacon around the beef. Sprinkle over the remaining salt.
4. Spoon the ricotta mixture down the center of the beef. Use the plastic wrap to bring the sides up and around the filling to create a cylinder. Press the sides together to seal—place on a plate, seam side down, and chill for an hour.
5. Place the fatty in the smoker and cook for two hours or until the bacon is completely brown. You may need to turn the fatty as it cooks. Take the fatty out of the smoker and allow to rest for 5 minutes before slicing and serving.

CHAPTER 2
PORK

DRY-RUBBED SMOKED RIBS - 31
GOCHUJANG PORK TENDERLOIN - 33
HAWAIIN PULLED PORK - 35
PEACH BARBECUE PULLED PORK - 37
PORK CHOPS - 39
SMOKED HAM WITH BROWN SUGAR GLAZE - 41
TWICE-SMOKED SPIRAL HAM - 43
CRISP 'N STICKY SMOKED SPARE RIBS - 45

DRY-RUBBED SMOKED RIBS

(TOTAL COOK TIME 1 HOUR 25 MINUTES)

INGREDIENTS FOR 6 SERVINGS

THE MEAT

- 1 rack baby back ribs

THE INGREDIENTS

- Olive oil – 2 tablespoons
- Smoked paprika – 1½ teaspoons
- Cayenne – 1 teaspoon
- Garlic powder – 1½ teaspoons
- Salt – 2 teaspoons
- Red pepper flakes – ½ teaspoon
- Italian herb seasoning – 1 teaspoon
- Brown sugar - ⅓ cup

THE SMOKE

- Set the smoker to 225°F (105°C) for indirect smoking

METHOD

1. Prepare the ribs by rinsing them and patting dry. Take a sharp paring knife and remove the silverskin.
2. Drizzle the ribs with oil.
3. Mix the smoked paprika, cayenne, garlic powder, salt, black pepper, red pepper flakes, Italian seasoning, and brown sugar. in a small bowl. Rub the mixture over the entire rack of ribs. Then wrap them in kitchen wrap, and transfer to the fridge for a minimum of 60 minutes.
4. Remove the ribs from the kitchen wrap and place them on the preheated smoker grate. Close the smoker's lid and smoke slowly for 4-6 minutes or until the internal temperature registers 145°F (60°C).
5. Take the ribs out from the smoker and transfer to a platter. Tent the platter with foil and allow to rest for 4-6 minutes.
6. Serve and enjoy.

GOCHUJANG PORK TENDERLOIN

(TOTAL COOK TIME 9 HOURS 40 MINUTES)

INGREDIENTS FOR 4 SERVINGS

THE MEAT

- 1 pork tenderloin

THE INGREDIENTS

- Gochujang sauce – ½ cup
- Green onions – 2 tablespoons
- Sesame seeds – 1 tablespoon

THE SMOKE

- Set the smoker to 225°F (105°C)

METHOD

1. Add the pork tenderloin in a large ziplock bag.
2. Pour the Gochujang sauce into the bag and allow to marinate for 8 hours.
3. Remove the meat from the marinade and shake off any excess.
4. Place the tenderloin directly on the grate and smoke for 60-90 minutes or until the meat registers an internal temperature of 150°F (65°C).
5. Remove the meat from the smoker and wrap in aluminum foil. Set aside to rest for 10 minutes before slicing.
6. Garnish with green onions and sesame seeds and enjoy.

HAWAIIN PULLED PORK

(TOTAL COOK TIME 14 HOURS 20 MINUTES)

INGREDIENTS FOR 18-20 SERVINGS

THE SEAFOOD

- 1 pork shoulder (6-lb, 2.7-kg)

THE CHEESE SAUCE

- Butter – 1 tablespoon
- Flour – 1 tablespoon
- Milk – ¾ cup
- BBQ rub – 1 tablespoon
- Cheese, shredded – 2 cups

THE INGREDIENTS

- Olive oil – 1 tablespoon
- Pork and poultry BBQ rub, any brand – 3 tablespoons
- Pineapple juice, divided (24-oz, 600-gm)

THE SMOKE

- Set the smoker to 225°F (130°C)
- Cherry wood pellets are a good choice for this recipe

METHOD

1. For the cheese sauce, melt the butter in a pan, add the flour and combine. Pour in the milk and mix well.
2. To the butter mixture, stir in the BBQ rub and incorporate.
3. Begin adding the cheese to the butter mixture, in one handful amount, until you achieve your preferred consistency.
4. For the pulled pork, first rub olive oil all over the meat.
5. Rub the BBQ seasoning all over and into the pork shoulder to cover.
6. Place the should on the smoker and cook for 3 hours. After which, spritz the meat with 1 cup of pineapple juice and ½ teaspoon of BBQ rub. Continue with this process every 60 minutes.
7. When the pork shoulder registers an internal temperature of 160°F (70°C) take it out of the smoke and wrap it with a double layer of aluminum foil. Before tightly sealing the foil, pour over ½ cup of pineapple juice.
8. Continue cooking the pork until it registers an internal temperature of 205°F (100°C). Once it does, remove it from the smoker and place in a cooler along with some tea towels. Rest the pork in the cooker for a minimum of 1½ hours before shredding.
9. Serve the pulled pork with a side of cheesy sauce.

PEACH BARBECUE PULLED PORK

(TOTAL COOK TIME 5 HOURS 15 MINUTES)

INGREDIENTS FOR 20 SERVINGS

THE MEAT

- Pork shoulder (10-lb, 4.5-kg)

THE INGREDIENTS

- Pork rub, any brand – 1 cup
- Peach BBQ sauce, any brand, as needed
- 20 sandwich buns, split
- Coleslaw, as needed

THE SMOKE

- Set the smoker to 350°F (175°C) for indirect smoking
- Hickory or pecan wood chips work well for this recipe

METHOD

1. Using kitchen paper towels, pat the meat dry.
2. Take a sharp knife and make cuts all over the surface of the butt. Scatter the pork rub over the pork, pressing it gently into the meat.
3. Cook the meat over indirect fire at around 250-300°F (120- 150°C) with the lid closed.
4. Cook the pork for around 5 hours, or until the internal temperature of the meat registers an internal temperature of 195-205°F (90-100°C) until the meat falls apart.
5. Remove from the smoker and set aside to rest for 20 minutes before shredding.
6. Mix 10 cups of sauce into the pulled, shredded pork.
7. Cook over moderate heat until heated through.
8. Serve the pulled pork in the sandwich buns topped with coleslaw.
9. Enjoy.

PORK CHOPS

(TOTAL COOK TIME 1 HOUR 45 MINUTES)

INGREDIENTS FOR 4 SERVINGS

THE MEAT

- 4 pork chops 1-in (1-cm) thick

THE RUB

- Black pepper – 1 tablespoon
- Paprika – 1 tablespoon
- Brown sugar – 1 tablespoon
- Kosher salt – 1½ teaspoons
- Dry mustard – ½ teaspoon
- Cayenne pepper – ¼ teaspoon

THE SMOKE

- Set the smoker to 225°F (105°C)
- Add your choice of wood chips to the wood tray

METHOD

1. In a bowl, combine the rub ingredients (black pepper, paprika, brown sugar, kosher salt, dry mustard, and cayenne pepper).
2. Pat the pork chops dry with a kitchen paper towel and scatter the rub generously over the meat, patting it in. Set the pork chops to one side at room temperature for 30 minutes.
3. Place the chops directly on the grate and cook for around 1 hour 15 minutes, or until the meat registers an internal temperature of 145°F (60°C).
4. Halfway through the cooking progress, turn the chops over.
5. Remove from the smoker and allow to rest for 5 minutes before enjoying.

SMOKED HAM WITH BROWN SUGAR GLAZE

(TOTAL COOK TIME 4 HOURS 10 MINUTES)

INGREDIENTS FOR 8-10 SERVINGS

THE MEAT

- 1 bone-in ham (7-lb, 3.5-kg)

THE INGREDIENTS

- Nonstick cooking spray
- BBQ rub, any brand – ⅓ cup
- Apple cider, divided – 2¼ cups
- Fresh herbs, of choice, to garnish, optional
- Fresh fruit, of choice, to garnish, optional

THE GLAZE

- Butter – ½ cup
- Brown sugar – ½ cup
- Maple syrup – ¼ cup

THE SMOKE

- Set the smoker to 250°F (120°C)
- Cherry wood chips are a good choice for this recipe

METHOD

1. Coat an aluminum foil pan with nonstick cooking spray.
2. Lay the ham, cut side facing down in the foil pan.
3. Scatter the BBQ rub over the surface of the meant.
4. Transfer the foil pan to the smoker and cook for 60 minutes.
5. Continue cooking the ham for an additional 2-3 hours, basting every 30-40 minutes with the 2 cups of cider. The ham is good to go when it registers an internal temperature of 140°F (60°C).
6. Meanwhile, prepare the glaze. Over moderate heat, combine the butter, brown sugar, syrup, and remaining apple cider in a pan. Bring to a simmer and cook until the glaze has thickened, for 6-8 minutes.
7. Brush the glaze over the surface of the ham. Transfer to a platter and garnish with herbs and fresh fruit.
8. Enjoy.

TWICE-SMOKED SPIRAL HAM

(TOTAL COOK TIME 3 HOURS 20 MINUTES)

INGREDIENTS FOR 10-12 SERVINGS

THE MEAT

- 1 smoked spiral ham, netting, and packaging removed (8-10-lb, 4-6-kg)

THE GLAZE

- Ginger ale – 2¼ cups
- Packed brown sugar – 1 cup
- Dijon mustard – 1½ teaspoons
- Runny honey – 3 tablespoons
- Apple cider vinegar – 4½ teaspoons
- 2 garlic cloves, peeled and minced

THE SMOKE

- Set the smoker to 240°F (110°C)
- Cherry wood chips are a good choice for this recipe

METHOD

1. For the glaze. In a small pan, combine the ginger ale with the brown sugar, Dijon mustard, honey, and apple cider vinegar, and bring to a boil. Cook for around 15 minutes until the glaze is reduced by half. Then stir in the garlic and cook for another 5 minutes. Remove the glaze from the heat.
2. Place the ham in a large aluminum foil pan. One by one, pull the slices apart and drizzle some of the glaze over the exposed meat. Take care not to tear any of the meat. Then, brush any remaining glaze over the surface of the meat.
3. Transfer the foil pan to the smoker and close the lid. You will need to baste the ham every 60 minutes or so with the glaze. The total smoking time is around 3 hours.
4. Serve and enjoy.

CRISP 'N STICKY SMOKED SPARE RIBS

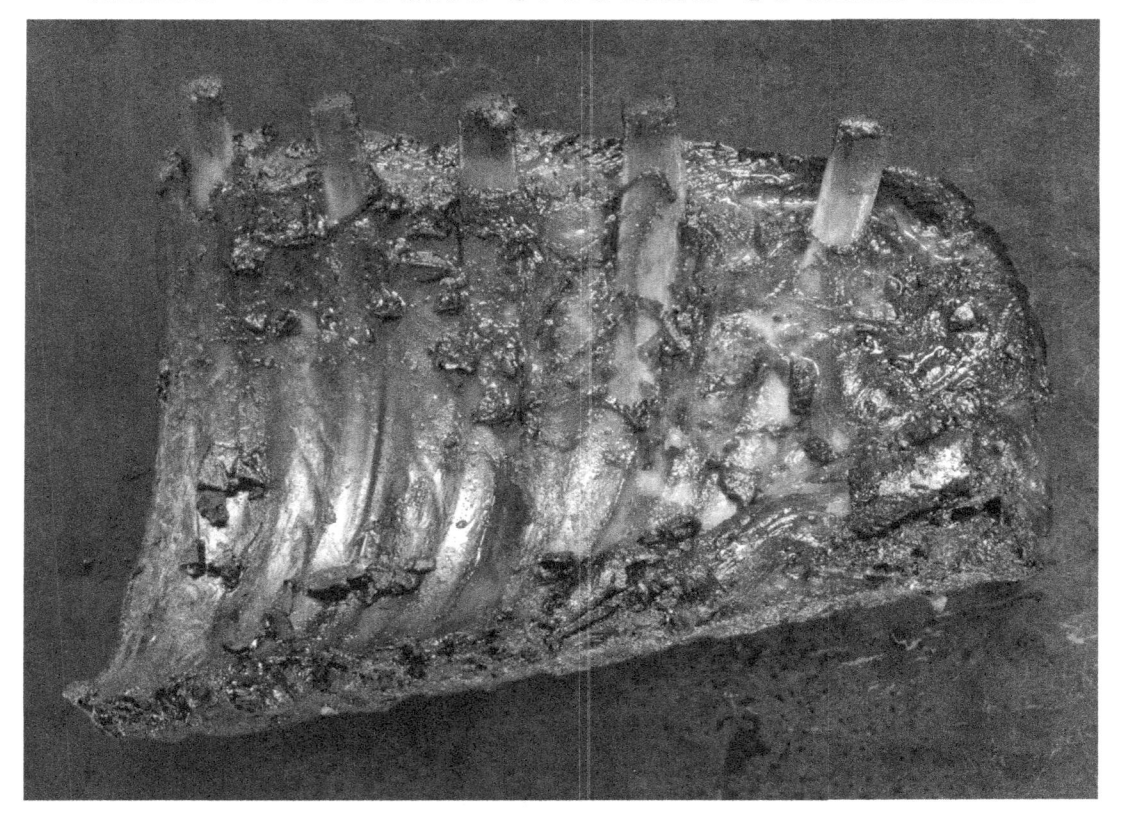

(TOTAL COOK TIME 5 HOURS 40 MINUTES)

INGREDIENTS FOR 4 SERVINGS

THE MEAT

- 1 rack of spare ribs, membrane removed

THE SEASONING

- Sweet rub, as needed, to season

THE LIQUID

- Brown sugar – ½ cup
- Butter, cubed – ½ cup
- Sour cherry juice – ½ cup

THE GLAZE

- Sour cherry juice – 1 cup
- Brown sugar – ½ cup
- Sweet rub, store-bought – 1 tablespoon

THE SMOKE

- Preheat the smoker to 225°F (110°C)
- Use cherry wood chips

METHOD

1. Prepare the ribs by trimming off any fat from the top and thin ribs at the end of the rack.
2. Season the ribs on both sides with sweet rub.
3. Transfer to the smoker, close its lid, and smoke the ribs for 4 hours.
4. Lay a large sheet of foil on a chopping board.
5. Scatter brown sugar, butter cubes, and sour cherry juice on the foil.
6. Place the ribs on top of the sugar-cherry juice mixture, bone side facing upwards. Close the foil securely around the ribs.
7. Return the ribs to the smoker, smoke for 60 minutes, or until the internal temperature registers 200°F (95°C).
8. Combine the glaze ingredients (sour cherry juice, brown sugar, and sweet rub) in a pan.
9. Take the ribs out of the foil and place on a chopping board. Pour any residual liquid from the foil into the glaze. Bring the glaze to a boil and cook for around 2-3 minutes.
10. Meanwhile, slice the ribs.
11. Dip each rib into the glaze and place on a baking sheet.
12. Increase the smoker heat to 450°F (230°C), and grill for 2-3 minutes on each side until the glaze is caramelized, and the edges are crisp.
13. Serve and enjoy.

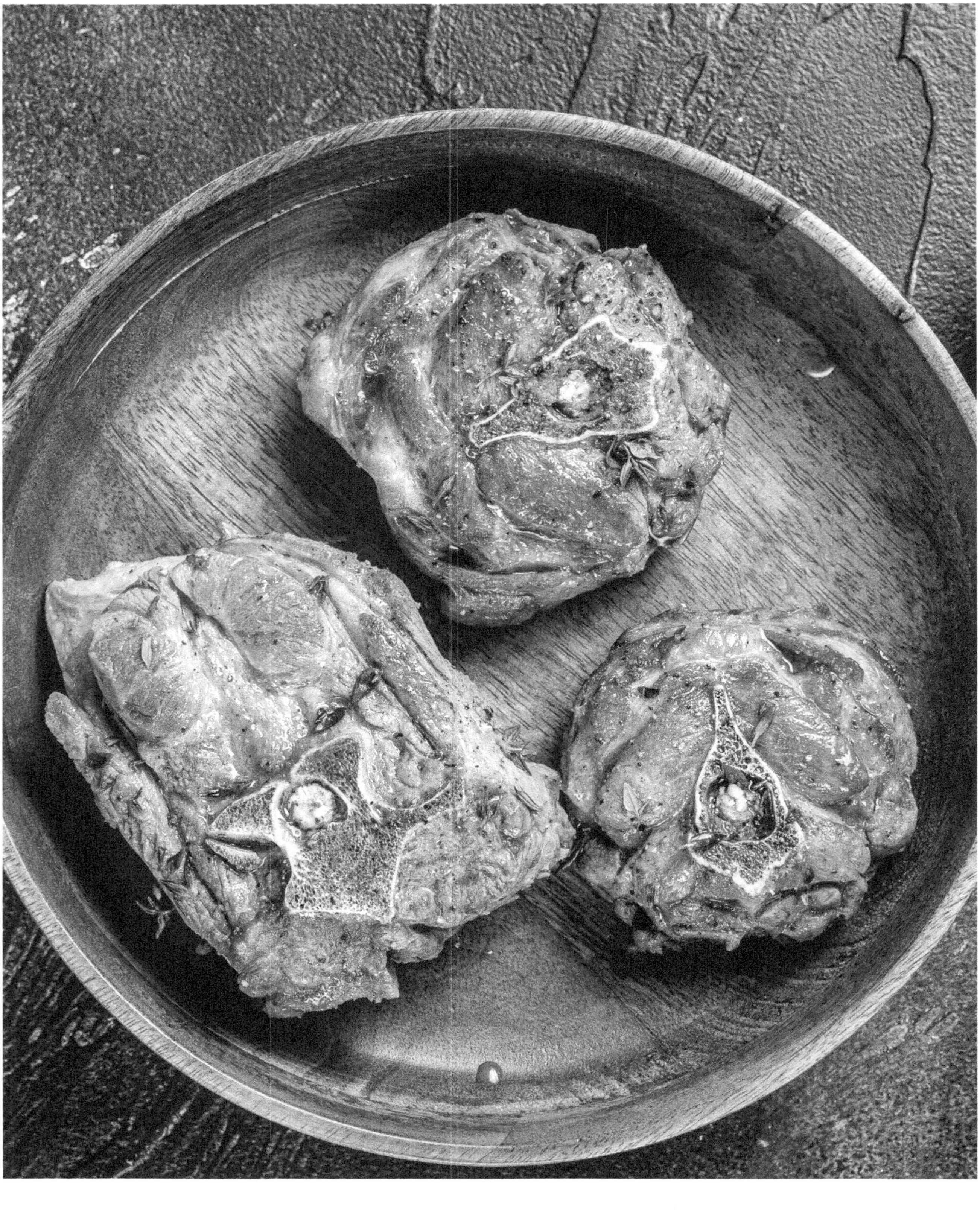

CHAPTER 3
LAMB

HICKORY SMOKED LAMB NECK - 51
LAMB SHOULDER - 53
SMOKED LEG OF LAMB - 55
RACK OF LAMB - 57
SMOKED LAMB SHANK - 59
GREEK LAMB WRAPS - 61

CUTS OF LAMB

HICKORY SMOKED LAMB NECK

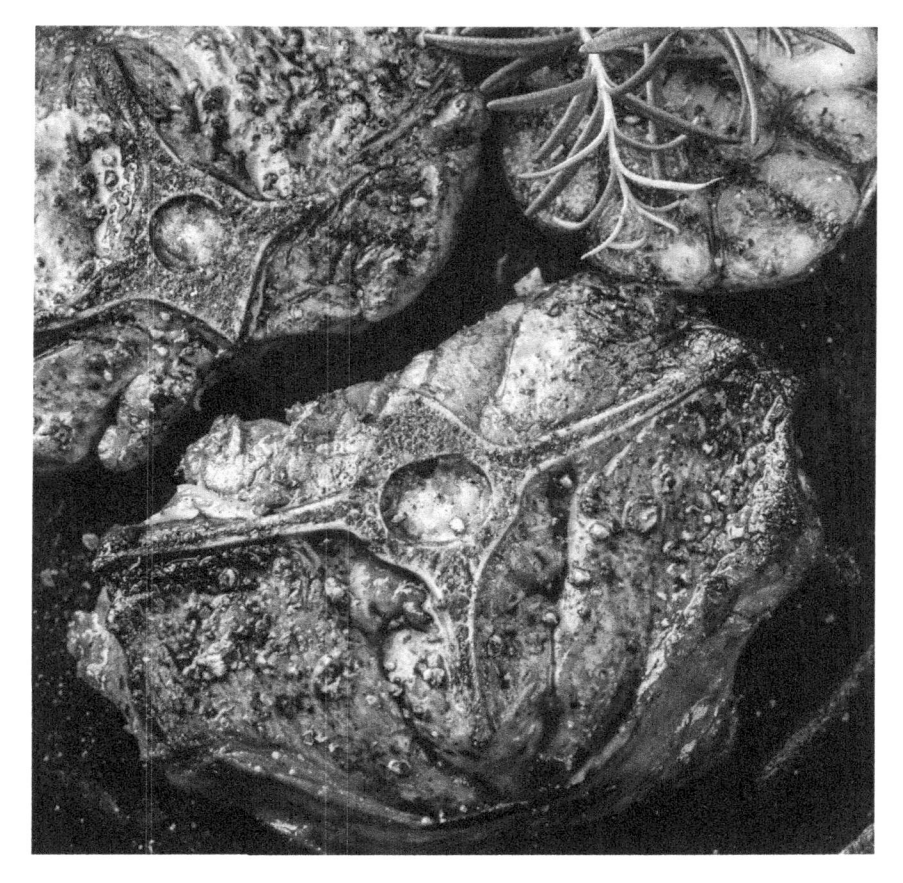

(TOTAL COOK TIME 11 HOURS 30 MINUTES)

INGREDIENTS FOR 4 SERVINGS

THE MEAT

- Lamb neck (2-lb, 0.9-kg)

THE BRINE

- Water – 8 cups
- Kosher salt – ½ cup

THE DRY RUB

- Dried rosemary – 1 tablespoon
- Dried thyme – 1 tablespoon
- Ground black pepper – 1 teaspoon
- Garlic salt – 1 teaspoon

THE SMOKE

- Set the smoker to 250°F (120°C)
- Hickory wood chips work well for this recipe

METHOD

1. For the wet brine, add the water and salt to a bucket, and stir until the salt dissolves.
2. Place the lamb in the bucket and submerge in the brine. Transfer the bucket to the fridge and leave overnight.
3. The following day remove the meat from the brine and rinse with cold water. Pat dry with kitchen paper towels.
4. Slice the lamb into steaks on less than 0.5-in (1-cm) thick.
5. Mix the dry rub ingredients (dried rosemary, thyme, black pepper, and salt) in a bowl. Crush any lumps with a fork.
6. Apply a liberal amount of the rub over the lamb, covering on all sides and into any folds.
7. Place the lamb on your smoker's grates and close the lid.
8. Smoke the lamb for around 2½ hours until the meat registers an internal temperature of 145°F (65°C).
9. Remove the lamb from the smoker and tent it loosely in foil. Set aside to rest for 20-30 minutes.
10. Serve and enjoy.

LAMB SHOULDER

(TOTAL COOK TIME 5 HOURS 30 MINUTES)

INGREDIENTS FOR 4 SERVINGS

THE MEAT

- Lamb shoulder, excess fat trimmed (3-lb, 1.5-kg)
- Apple juice, to spritz

THE DRY RUB

- Brown sugar – 1½ cups
- 4 sprigs of fresh rosemary
- Kosher salt - ⅓ cup
- Cayenne pepper – 2 tablespoons
- Freshly ground black pepper – 1 tablespoon
- Ground cumin – 1 tablespoon

THE SMOKE

- Set the smoker to 250°F (120°C)
- Choose your favorite wood chips for this recipe

METHOD

1. Trim the excess fat from the meat, rinse under cold running water, and with kitchen paper towels, pat dry.
2. Next, prepare the dry rub. In a small bowl, combine the brown sugar, fresh rosemary, salt, cayenne pepper, black pepper, and ground cumin. Using a fork, break up any lumps.
3. Apply the lamb liberally all over the meat, working into the folds. Set aside for around 30 minutes at room temperature.
4. Place the lamb on the smoker's grates, shoulder fat facing up and bone down. Close the smoker's lid and smoke for 2 hours before spritzing with apple juice, and then after every 30-60 minutes. The total smoking time is around 5 hours until the meat registers an internal temperature of 165°F (75°C).
5. Next, spritz the meat again with apple juice and wrap in foil. Then increase the smoker temperature to 300°F (150°C). Return to the smoker and continue to smoke until the meat registers 195°F (90°C).
6. Remove the meat from the smoker and tent loosely in foil. Set aside for 30 minutes before slicing.
7. Enjoy.

SMOKED LEG OF LAMB

(TOTAL COOK TIME 4 HOURS 10 MINUTES)

INGREDIENTS FOR 8 SERVINGS

THE MEAT

- Leg of lamb, excess fat trimmed, silverskin removed (6-lb, 2.7-kg)
- Yellow mustard – 2 tablespoons

THE DRY RUB

- Kosher salt– 1 tablespoon
- Black pepper – 2 teaspoons
- Granulated garlic – 1 teaspoon
- Rosemary – 1 teaspoon
- Thyme – 1 teaspoon
- Brown sugar – 1 teaspoon
- Paprika – ½ teaspoon

THE SMOKE

- Set the smoker to 250°F (120°C)
- You will need 2 pieces of fruit flavored wood for this recipe

METHOD

1. Combine all the rub ingredients in a bowl, breaking up any lumps with a fork.
2. Rub a fine layer of yellow mustard over the lamb.
3. Scatter the rub over the mustard, making sure it is evenly covered.
4. Transfer the lamb to the smoker, and smoke for 4 hours, or until the meat registers an internal temperature of 150°F (65°C).
5. Remove the lamb from the smoker and allow to rest for 10 minutes before slicing.
6. Serve and enjoy.

RACK OF LAMB

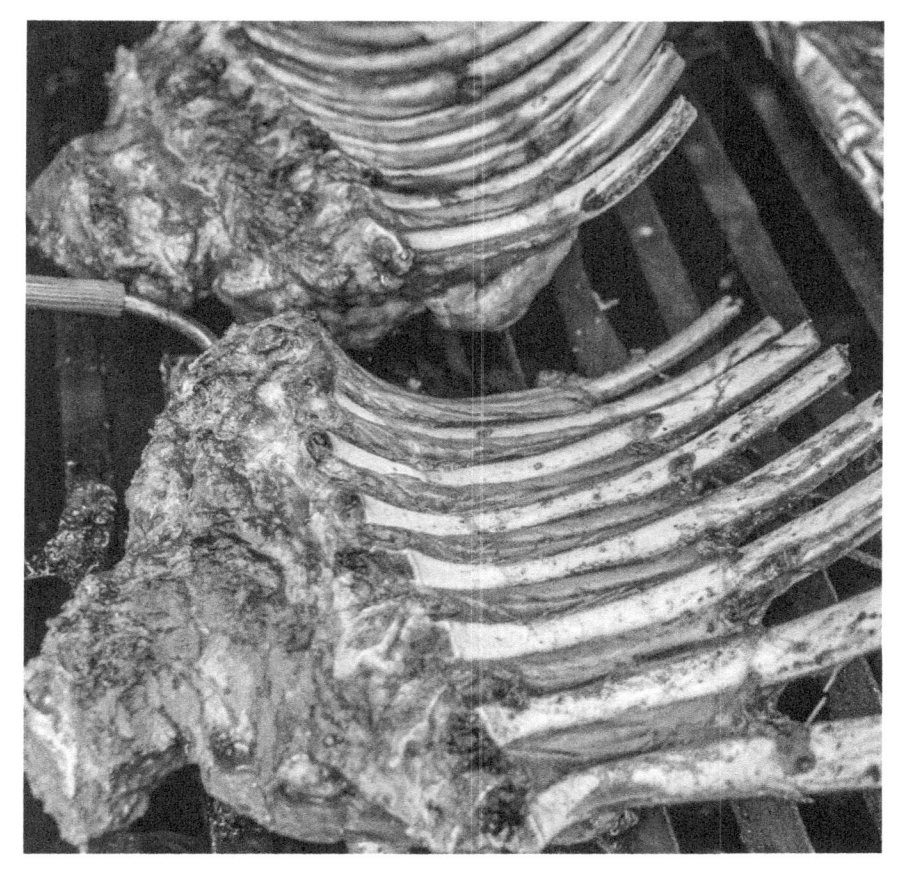

(TOTAL COOK TIME 1 HOUR 20 MINUTES)

INGREDIENTS FOR 4 SERVINGS

THE MEAT

- Rack of lamb (2-lb, 0.9-kg)
- Olive oil, as needed

THE DRY RUB

- Ground white pepper – 2 tablespoons
- Smoked paprika – 2 tablespoons
- Freshly ground black pepper – 2 tablespoons
- Ground chipotle pepper – 2 tablespoons
- Onion powder – 1½ tablespoons
- Kosher salt – 1 tablespoon
- Garlic powder – 1½ tablespoon
- Ground cumin – 2 teaspoons

THE SMOKE

- Set the smoker to 225-250°F (105-120°C)
- Hickory wood chips work well for this recipe

METHOD

1. For the dry rub, combine the white pepper, paprika, black pepper, chipotle pepper, onion powder, kosher salt, garlic powder, and ground cumin. Using a fork, crush any lumps.
2. Spread a fine layer of oil over the rack of lamb, and scatter over a generous amount of the dry rub to cover all sides.
3. Place the rack fat side facing up on the smoker's grates. Add the wood chips and close the lid. Smoke the rack for 60 minutes until the meat registers an internal temperature of 135°F (55°C).
4. Take the meat out of the smoker and transfer it to a cutting board for 10 minutes, to rest.
5. Carve into single chops and enjoy.

SMOKED LAMB SHANK

(TOTAL COOK TIME 4 HOURS 40 MINUTES)

INGREDIENTS FOR 4 SERVINGS

THE MEAT

- 4 lamb shanks, trimmed of fat, and silverskin, rinsed and patted dry

THE DRY RUB

- Kosher salt – ½ cup
- Freshly ground black pepper – ½ cup

THE BRAISE

- Beef broth - 2 cups
- 4 sprigs of rosemary
- 2 white onions, chopped
- 4 medium carrots, sliced into rounds
- Red wine – 4 cups

THE SMOKE

- Set the smoker to 225°F (105°C)
- Hickory wood chips work well for this recipe

METHOD

1. For the dry rub, combine the salt with the pepper, and crush any lumps with a fork.
2. Apply a liberal amount of the dry rub to the meat, covering all sides and into the folds.
3. Place the meat on the smoker grates and close the lid. Cook the meat until it registers an internal temperature of 160°F (70°C) for approximately 2 hours.
4. Remove the lamb shanks from the smoker and transfer to an aluminum foil pan.
5. Prepare the braise. Combine the broth, rosemary, onions, carrots, and wine in a bowl.
6. Next, pour the braising liquid over the lamb shanks. Then wrap the pan tightly in foil and return to the smoker.
7. Smoke the lamb until it registers an internal temperature of 195°F (90°C) for around 2 hours.
8. Remove the meat from the smoker and leave it in the aluminum foil to rest for 25-30 minutes before enjoying.

GREEK LAMB WRAPS

(TOTAL COOK TIME 2 HOURS 25 MINUTES)

INGREDIENTS FOR 4-6 SERVINGS

THE MEAT

- 1 leg of lamb, room temperature (6-lbs, 2.7-kgs)

THE INGREDIENTS

- Freshly squeezed juice of 1 lemon
- Olive oil
- Big game rub, as needed
- 12 pita
- 3 Roma tomatoes, sliced
- 1 Spanish red onion, peeled, halved and sliced into half-moons
- Feta cheese, crumbled (8-ozs, 227-gms)

TZATZIKI

- Plain Greek yogurt – 2 cups
- 2 English cucumbers, seeded and finely chopped
- 2 garlic cloves, peeled, and finely minced
- Zest of 2 lemons
- Fresh dill – 4 tablespoons
- Mint – 2 tablespoons
- Sea salt, to taste
- Freshly ground black pepper, to taste

THE SMOKE

- When you are ready to cook: with the lid open, establish the fire, for 4-5 minutes
- Preheat to 400°F (200°C) with the lid closed, for 12-15 minutes
- Use apple wood chips

METHOD

1. Rub the lamb all over first with the fresh lemon juice and then with the oil. Season well with the game rub.
2. Roast in the smoker for half an hour. Turn the heat down to 350 °F (180°C) and continue cooking until the meat registers (for medium-rare) an internal temperature of 140°F (60°C).
3. In the meantime, prepare the tzatziki: In a bowl, combine all the ingredients (yogurt, cucumber, garlic, lemon zest, fill, mint, salt, black pepper) mixing well to combine.
4. Transfer to the fridge to chill.
5. Place the pita on the grill to warm through.
6. Place the lamb on a chopping board and allow to rest for 15 minutes before diagonally slicing into thin slices.
7. To assemble the wraps: Fill the warmed pita with the sliced lamb, add a dollop of tzatziki and fill with tomato, red onions, and crumbled feta.
8. Serve and enjoy.

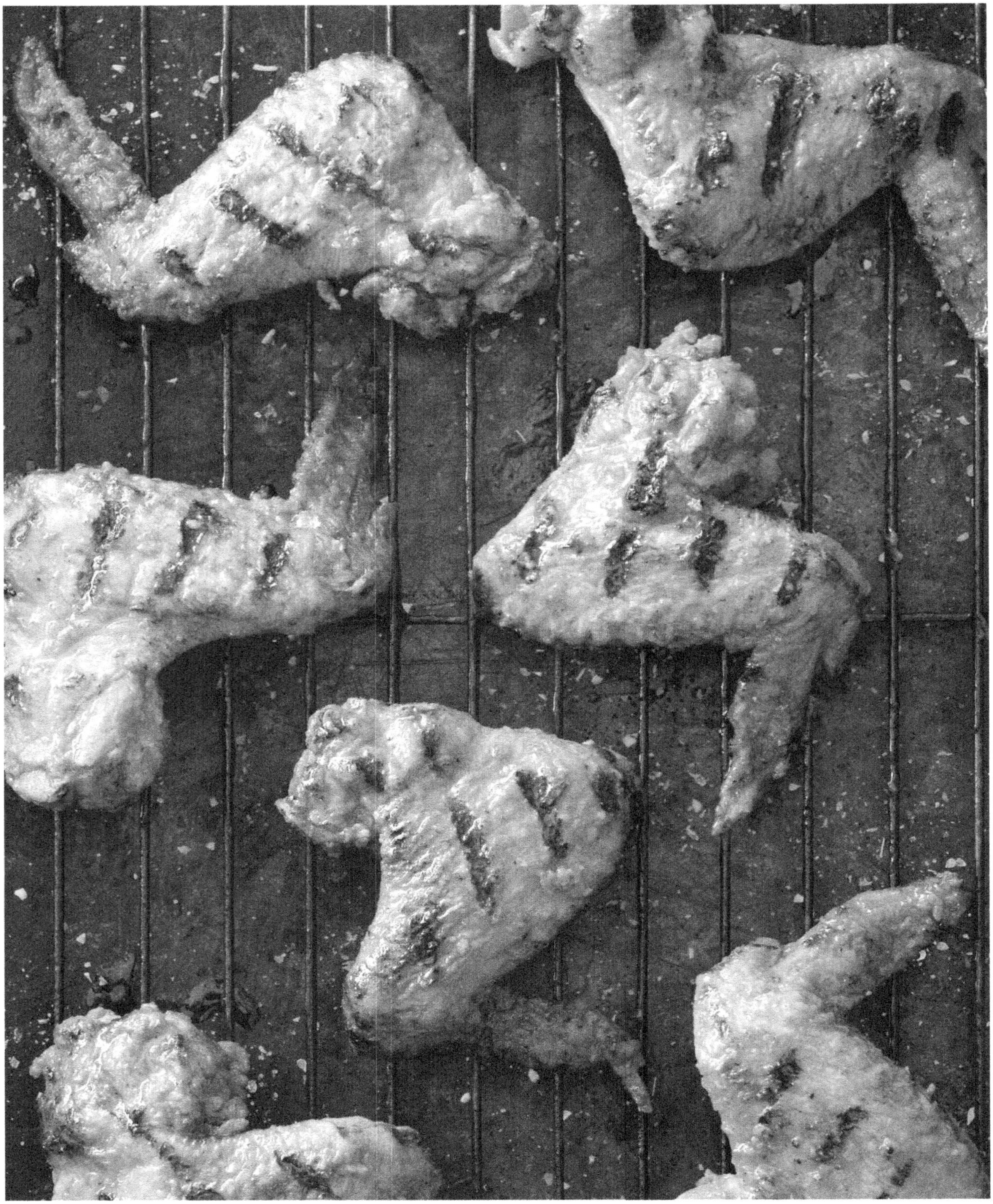

CHAPTER 4
CHICKEN

HULI HULI HAWAIIN-STYLE CHICKEN - 67
SMOKED BACON-WRAPPED CHICKEN BREASTS - 70
SMOKED CHICKEN LEGS - 72
WHOLE SMOKED CHICKEN - 74
BBQ CHICKEN LOLLIPOPS - 76
CHERRY COLA CHICKEN WINGS - 78
BACON-WRAPPED, MUSHROOM STUFFED CHICKEN THIGHS - 80

CUTS OF CHICKEN

HULI HULI HAWAIIN-STYLE CHICKEN

(TOTAL COOK TIME 2 HOURS)

INGREDIENTS FOR 5 SERVINGS

THE MEAT

- Chicken breast, cubed (2-lb, 0.9-kg)

THE INGREDIENTS

- Fresh pineapple, peeled, cored, and cubed
- Bell peppers, chopped into chunks – 3 cups
- Onion, peeled and chopped into chunks – 2 cups
- 1 large zucchini, cut into slices 0.5-in (1-cm) thick

THE MARINADE

- Soy sauce – 1 cup
- Packed brown sugar – ½ cup
- 2 garlic cloves, peeled and minced
- Fresh ginger, peeled and grated – 1 teaspoon

THE HULI HULI SAUCE

- Cornstarch – 1 tablespoon
- Water – 1½ tablespoons
- Ketchup – ⅓ cup
- Apple cider vinegar – ⅓ cup
- Pineapple juice – ½ cup
- Orange juice – 2 tablespoons
- Orange zest – ½ teaspoon
- Fresh ginger, grated – ½ teaspoon
- 3 garlic cloves, peeled and finely minced

THE SMOKE

- Set the smoker to moderately high heat

METHOD

1. Add the chicken to a large resealable bag.
2. For the marinade, combine the ingredients in a bowl. Pour the marinade into the bag and over the chicken. Toss to coat, squeeze out the air, and marinade for 60 minutes.
3. In a small bowl, prepare a slurry by combining the cornstarch with the water.
4. In a pan, for the sauce, combine the ketchup, vinegar, pineapple juice, orange juice, orange zest, ginger, and garlic. Place over moderate heat and bring to a boil. Turn the heat down to low and stir in the slurry. Whisk the mixture until it thickens, cover, and keep warm.
5. Skewer the chicken and the veggies, and grill until the meat registers an internal temperature of 165°F (75°C) and the veggies are tender.
6. Remove from the smoker and enjoy with huli huli sauce.

SMOKED BACON-WRAPPED CHICKEN BREASTS

(TOTAL COOK TIME 3 HOURS 25 MINUTES)

INGREDIENTS FOR 6 SERVINGS

THE MEAT

- 6 chicken breasts

THE INGREDIENTS

- BBQ dry rub, any brand – ¼ cup
- 12 bacon slices

THE BRINE

- Water – 4 cups
- Kosher salt – ¼ cup
- Brown sugar – ¼ cup
- Black peppercorns – ½ teaspoon
- 4 garlic cloves, peeled and crushed

THE SMOKE

- Set the smoker to 275°F (135°C)
- Cherry wood is a good choice for this recipe

METHOD

1. In a pan, bring the brine ingredients to a boil (water, kosher salt, brown sugar, peppercorns, and garlic) and cook until the salt and sugar are dissolved. Remove from the heat and allow to cool completely.
2. Pour the brine into a large ziplock bag. Add the chicken to the bag, remove as much air as possible, and seal. Transfer to the fridge for 2 hours, flipping the bag over to ensure consistent brining.
3. Take the chicken out of the brine, and rinse under cold running water.
4. Apply a liberal amount of BBQ rub to the breast to coat fully.
5. Place 2 bacon slices on a chopping board. Place one chicken breast on top, and beginning at one end, wrap the bacon tightly around the chicken breast. Secure each end with a cocktail stick. Repeat the process with the remaining chicken.
6. Smoke the chicken breast for 1-1½ hours or until it registers an internal temperature of 165°F (75°C). Flip over once halfway through the smoking process.
7. Remove the bacon-wrapped chicken from the smoker and set it aside to rest for 5 minutes before serving.

SMOKED CHICKEN LEGS

(TOTAL COOK TIME 2 HOURS 35 MINUTES)

INGREDIENTS FOR 6 SERVINGS

THE MEAT

- Chicken legs (3-lb, 1.5-kg)

THE INGREDIENTS

- Olive oil – 3 tablespoons
- Poultry dry rub, any brand – as needed

THE SMOKE

- Set the smoker to 250°F (120°C)

METHOD

1. Add the chicken legs to a large ziplock bag.
2. Pour the olive oil into the bag, followed by a liberal amount of dry rub. Using clean hands, make sure the chicken legs are evenly coated. You may need to add more oil if necessary. Allow to rest for a minimum of 60 minutes.
3. Smoke the chicken legs for 1½-2 hours until the internal temperature registers 165°F (75°C).
4. Then preheat your broiler to high heat.
5. Place the chicken in the middle of the oven, skin side facing upwards, and broil for around 3 minutes until the fat crackles but the skin doesn't burn.
6. Enjoy.

WHOLE SMOKED CHICKEN

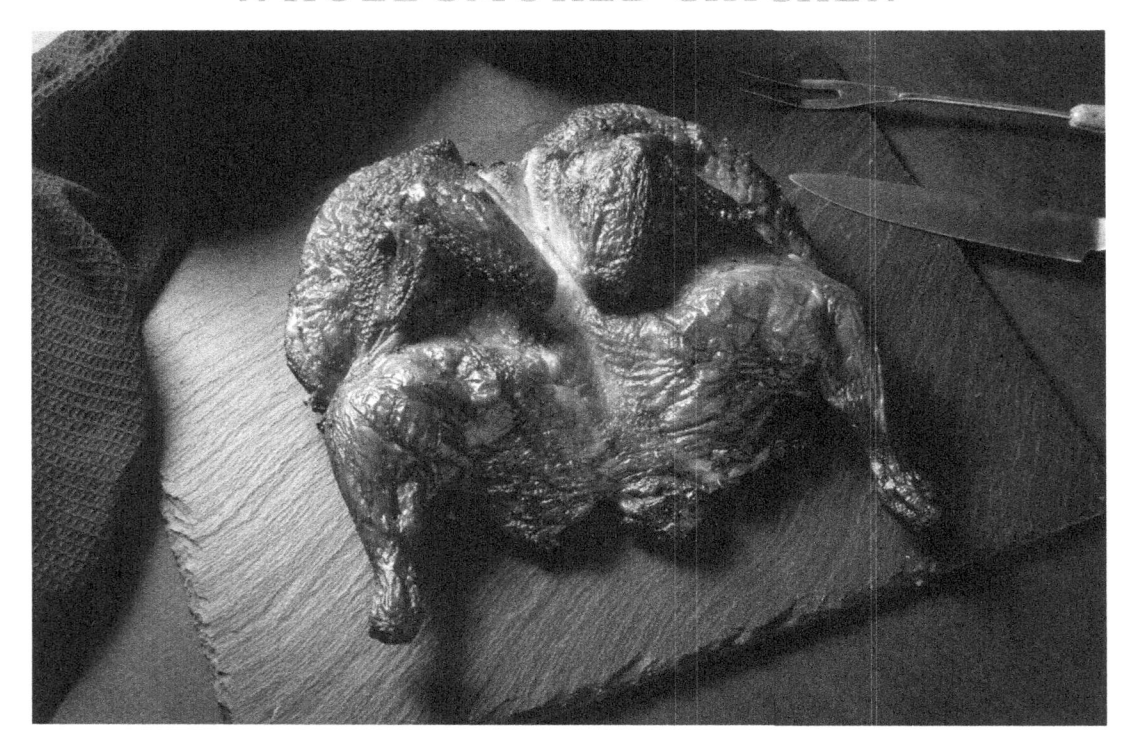

(TOTAL COOK TIME 6 HOURS)

INGREDIENTS FOR 6 SERVINGS

THE MEAT

- 1 roaster chicken, giblets removed (5-lb, 2-kg)

THE BRINE

- Water – 3-gal (11-lt)
- Kosher salt – 3 cups
- Apple juice – 4 cups
- Dark brown sugar – 2 cups

THE RUB

- Olive oil – 2 tablespoons
- Black pepper – 1 tablespoon
- Sea salt – 1 tablespoon
- Garlic powder – 2 teaspoons
- Parsley – 2 teaspoons

THE SMOKE

- Set the smoker to 225°F (105°C)

METHOD

1. Prepare the brine by combining the water, kosher salt, apple juice, and dark brown sugar in a large pot, and bring to a boil to dissolve the sugar and salt. Remove from the heat and set aside to cool completely.
2. Add the chicken to a large bowl, pour the cooled brine over the bird, and submerge. Allow to brine for 4-24 hours. Then, remove the chicken from the brine, and rinse with cooled fresh water.
3. Using kitchen paper, dry the chicken, and using kitchen twine tie its legs together.
4. Coat the chicken with the oil on both sides and between the skin and breast.
5. In a small bowl, combine the black pepper, sea salt, garlic powder, and parsley.
6. Season the bird with the rub.
7. Place the chicken on the grill rack, breast side facing up, and smoke for around 45 minutes. Increase the smoker's temperature to 400°F (200°C) and continue to cook until the internal temperature of the chicken registers 165°F (75°C), for around 45 minutes.
8. Remove the bird from the smoker and set it aside to rest for 10-15 minutes.
9. Serve and enjoy.

BBQ CHICKEN LOLLIPOPS

(TOTAL COOK TIME 50 MINUTES)

INGREDIENTS FOR 8-10 SERVINGS

THE MEAT

- Chicken drumsticks, Frenched (2-lb, 0.9-kg)

THE SEASONING

- BBQ rub, as needed

THE SAUCE

- BBQ sauce – ½ cup
- Ketchup – ½ cup
- Apple cider vinegar – ¼ cup
- Brown sugar – ½ cup
- BBQ rub – 2 tablespoons

THE SMOKE

- Preheat, the smoker to 365°F (185°C)
- Choose your favorite wood chips

METHOD

1. Wrap the bone end of each chicken drumstick with aluminum foil, and season the meat with BBQ rub.
2. Place the drumsticks directly on the smoker's grill grate, and cook for 10 minutes. Then, flip over and cook for another 10 minutes.
3. Meanwhile, prepare the sauce. In a bowl, combine the BBQ sauce, ketchup, apple cider vinegar, brown sugar, and BBQ rub.
4. When 20 minutes of smoking time has passed, check the internal temperature of the chicken. When the drumsticks register 165°F (75°C), dip each one in the sauce and return to the grill grates. Continue to cook until the internal temperature registers 175°F (80°C).
5. Serve and enjoy.

CHERRY COLA CHICKEN WINGS

(TOTAL COOK TIME 20 HOURS 20 MINUTES)

INGREDIENTS FOR 12 SERVINGS

THE MEAT

- Chicken wings, partitioned, tips discarded (4-lb, 1.8-kg)

THE BRINE

- Cherry cola – 4¼ cups
- Kosher salt – 2 tablespoons

THE INGREDIENTS

- BBQ rub – 4 tablespoons
- Brown sugar – 4 tablespoons
- Cornstarch – 4 tablespoons

THE SMOKE

- Preheat the smoker to 150°F (65°C)
- Choose your favorite wood chips

METHOD

1. Around 18 hours before you cook the wings, add them to a ziplock bag.
2. Pour in the cherry cola and 2 tablespoons of kosher salt.
3. Remove the wings from the brine, and pat dry with kitchen paper.
4. Transfer the wings to a very large bowl.
5. Add the BBQ rub, brown sugar, and cornstarch. Toss until well and evenly covered.
6. Smoke the wings for around 2 hours.
7. Remove from the smoker and enjoy.

BACON-WRAPPED, MUSHROOM STUFFED CHICKEN THIGHS

(TOTAL COOK TIME 2 HOURS 45 MINUTES)

INGREDIENTS FOR 4-8 SERVINGS

THE MEAT

- 8 chicken thighs, boneless and skinless
- 8 slices of bacon, regular thickness

THE STUFFING

- Butter – 2 tablespoons
- 1 onion, peeled and minced
- Mushrooms, chopped – 1 cup
- 2 cloves of garlic, peeled and minced
- Freshly parsley, chopped – ½ cup
- Salt and black pepper, to season

THE SMOKE

- Preheat, the smoker to 250°F (120°C)
- Use alder wood chips for this recipe

METHOD

1. Prepare the stuffing: Melt the butter in the pan and add the onions, mushrooms, and garlic. Cook until the onions are fork-tender.
2. Next, add the parsley and season with salt and pepper. Cook the mixture for an additional 2-3 minutes.
3. Take the stuffing off the heat and allow it to cool.
4. Lay a slice of bacon on a chopping board.
5. Place a chicken thigh on top of the slice of bacon. Spoon a small amount of the stuffing on the center of the chicken thigh. Wrap the bacon around the stuffing and secure with kitchen string.
6. Smoke the chicken thighs in the smoker for 2-2½ hours.
7. Transfer to the grill to crisp the bacon, if necessary.

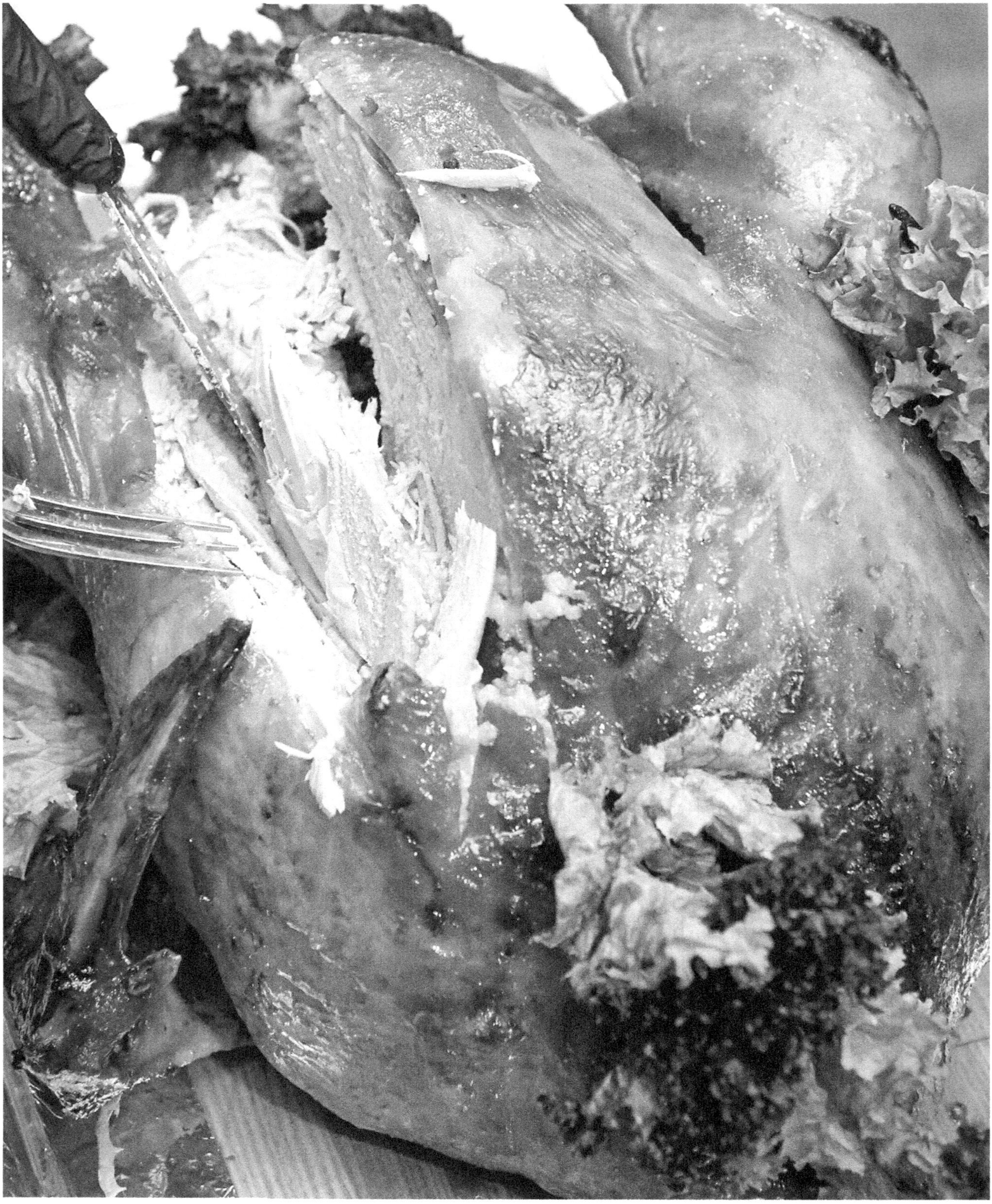

CHAPTER 5
TURKEY

BRINED AND SMOKED CITRUS TURKEY
BREAST - 85
CRISPY TURKEY WINGS - 88
THANKSGIVING TURKEY - 90
SIMPLE SMOKED TURKEY LEG - 92

CUTS OF TURKEY

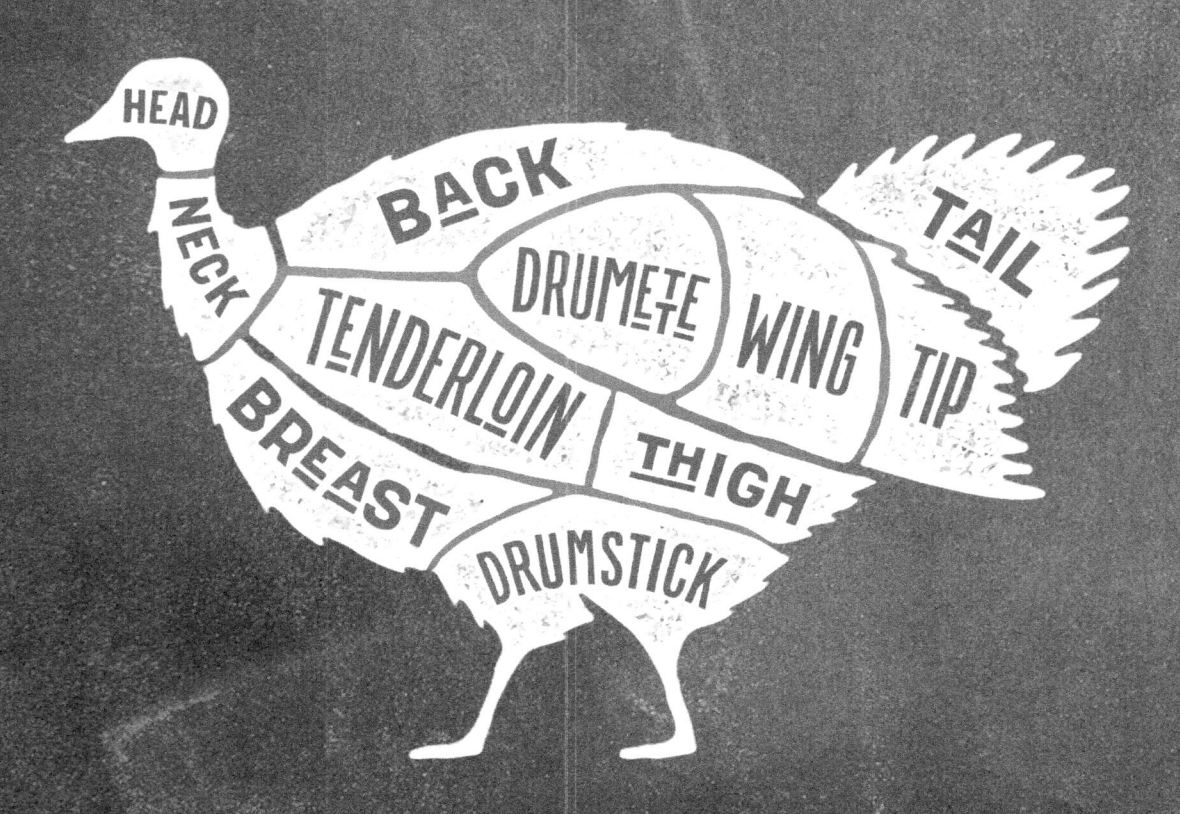

- HEAD
- NECK
- BACK
- TENDERLOIN
- BREAST
- DRUMETE
- WING
- TAIL
- TIP
- THIGH
- DRUMSTICK

BRINED AND SMOKED CITRUS TURKEY BREAST

(TOTAL COOK TIME 26 HOURS)

INGREDIENTS FOR 12 SERVINGS

THE MEAT

- 1 whole bone-in turkey breast, trimmed of ribs (8-lb, 4-kg)

THE BRINE

- Water – 4 cups
- 1 can frozen orange juice concentrate, thawed (12-oz, 350-gm)
- Kosher salt – ¾ cup
- Packed brown sugar – ½ cup
- 2 rosemary sprigs
- Black peppercorns – 2 tablespoons
- 2 fresh bay leaves
- 2 garlic cloves, peeled and smashed
- Ice cubes – 4 cups

THE INGREDIENTS

- 2 navel oranges, halved
- 2 limes, halved
- 2 lemons, halved
- Water, as needed

THE SMOKE

- Set the smoker to 225°F (105°C) for indirect heat
- Use hickory wood chips for this recipe and presoak for 3 hours before smoking

METHOD

1. In a big pot over moderately high heat, heat the water, orange juice, salt, brown sugar, rosemary, black peppercorns, bay leaves, and garlic, and bring to a boil. Cover the pot with a lid and remove from the heat. Allow to cool for around 20 minutes.
2. Then stir in the ice until it melts.
3. Juice the orange, limes, and lemons into the brine, and add their rinds.
4. Add the turkey to the citrus brine, skin side facing down. You may want to add more water to cover the breast and keep it submerged. Cover the pot and transfer to the fridge for 24-48 hours.
5. Prepare your smoker grill for indirect grilling. Heat one side to moderately high heat and keep the other side unlit.
6. Drain the wood chunks and place them in a disposable foil pan or smoker box over direct heat until smoldering.
7. Take the turkey out of the brine, pat dry, and place with the skin side facing upwards over indirect heat.
8. Covered, smoke the turkey until it registers an internal temperature of 165°F (75°C) for 1½-2 hours, rotating a ¼ turn every 20-25 minutes.
9. Allow the turkey to rest for around 30 minutes, and then carve.

CRISPY TURKEY WINGS

(TOTAL COOK TIME 2 HOURS 25 MINUTES)

INGREDIENTS FOR 4 SERVINGS

THE MEAT

- 1 whole or split turkey wings, patted dry (3-lb, 1.5-kg)

THE INGREDIENTS

- Olive oil – 2 tablespoons
- Brown sugar – 2 teaspoons
- Chili powder – 1 teaspoon
- Onion powder – ½ teaspoon
- Garlic powder – ½ teaspoon
- Smoked paprika – 1 teaspoon
- Salt and black pepper, to season

THE SMOKE

- Set the smoker to 225°F (105°C)

METHOD

1. Drizzle oil over the turkey wings.
2. Add the sugar, chili powder, onion powder, garlic powder, and smoked paprika to a bowl, and stir to combine. Scatter the seasoning over the wings to cover on both sides. Rub the mixture into the turkey wings and season with salt and black pepper.
3. Place the seasoned wings on the smoker and smoke until they reach an internal temperate of 165°F (75°C). This will take around 2 hours.
4. For crispy skin, increase the smoker temperature to 350°F (175°C), and smoke for 15-20 minutes, flipping over, until crisp.
5. Allow to cool before serving.

THANKSGIVING TURKEY

(TOTAL COOK TIME 8 HOURS 15 MINUTES)

INGREDIENTS FOR 8 SERVINGS

THE MEAT

- 1 turkey, giblets removed, bird rinsed (10-14-lb, 4-6-kg)

THE BRINE

- Water (3-gal, 11-L)
- Kosher salt – 3 cups
- Apple juice – 4 cups
- Dark brown sugar – 2 cups

THE SEASONED BUTTER

- 6 garlic cloves, peeled and minced
- Freshly cracked black pepper – 1 tablespoon
- Rosemary, chopped – 1 tablespoon
- Thyme, chopped – 1 tablespoon
- Sage, chopped – 1 tablespoon
- Salted butter – 1 cup

THE SMOKE

- Set the smoker to 225°F (105°C) for indirect heat

METHOD

1. In a big pot, combine the brine ingredients, and bring to a boil to dissolve the salt and sugar. Remove from the heat and allow to cool completely.
2. Submerge the turkey in the brine for 4-24 hours.
3. Remove the bird from the brine, and pat dry with kitchen paper. Tie the legs together with twine.
4. Add the dry seasoning ingredients (garlic, black pepper, rosemary, thyme, and sage) to the butter and mix thoroughly.
5. Rub the seasoning mixture over the surface, the sides, in between the skin and breast meat of the turkey.
6. Lay the bird directly, the breast side facing upwards, on a grill rack, and smoke for 3 hours.
7. Every 40-45 minutes, spritz the turkey with chicken broth every 45 minutes, starting after the first 60 minutes of cooking.
8. Turn the smoker temperature up to 350°F (175°C) and cook until the bird registers an internal temperature of 165°F (75°C) for another 60 minutes.
9. Remove the turkey from the smoker and allow to rest for 10-15 minutes before enjoying.

SIMPLE SMOKED TURKEY LEG

(TOTAL COOK TIME 2 HOURS 5 MINUTES)

INGREDIENTS FOR 4-6 SERVINGS

THE MEAT

- Turkey leg (1.5-lb, 0.7-kg)

THE INGREDIENTS

- Extra-virgin olive oil – 1 tablespoon
- Poultry rub – 2 tablespoons

THE SMOKE

- Preheat, the smoker to 250°F (120°C)
- Choose fruit wood chips

METHOD

1. Coat the turkey leg with oil and poultry rub.
2. Smoke the turkey leg for around 2 hours, or until the meat registers 160°F (70°C).
3. Remove from the smoker and serve.

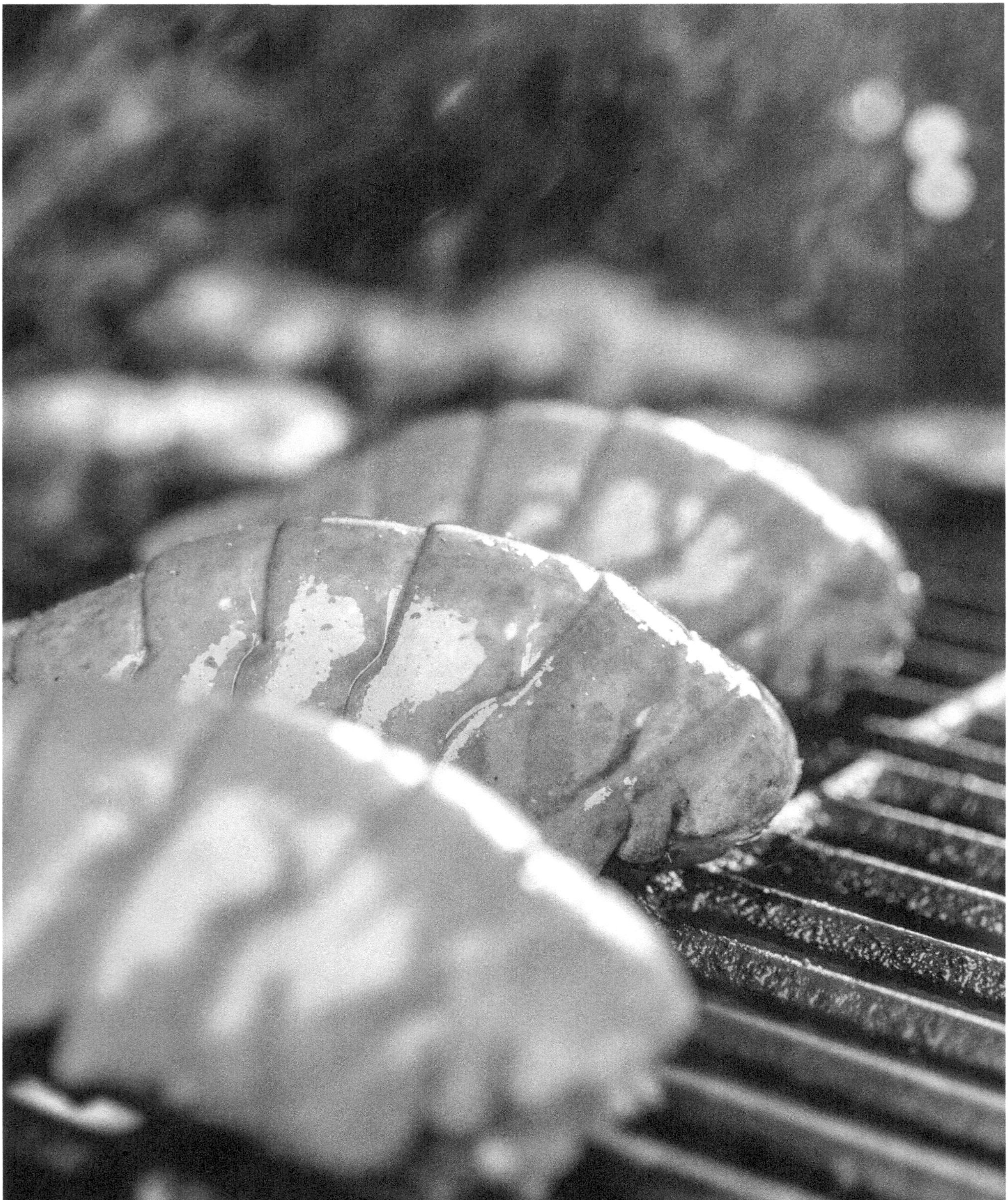

CHAPTER 6
SEAFOOD

GARLIC DILL SALMON - 97
PESTO TOPPED SALMON - 99
SALMON WITH BLUEBERRY AND GARLIC CHEESE SAUCE - 101
SMOKED CATFISH - 104
SPICY SMOKED TUNA - 106
TUNA STEAKS - 108
SMOKED CHILEAN SEA BASS - 110
SMOKED RAINBOW TROUT WITH LEMON DILL SAUCE - 112
CHERRY-SMOKED CLAMS IN WHITE WINE BUTTER SAUCE - 114
SMOKED CRAB CAKES - 116
SMOKED LOBSTER TAILS - 119
SMOKED SHRIMP IN CAJUN GARLIC BUTTER - 121
SMOKED OYSTERS WITH COMPOUND BACON- BUTTER - 124

CUTS OF CRAB
CLAW
CLAW
CLAW
CLAW
WHITE
WHITE
LUMP
LUMP
JUMBO LUMP
JUMBO LUMP
CLAW
CLAW

GARLIC DILL SALMON

(TOTAL COOK TIME 20 HOURS 15 MINUTES)

INGREDIENTS FOR 12 SERVINGS

THE FISH

- 2 large salmon fillets, pin bones removed

THE BRINE

- Water – 2 cups
- Brown sugar – 1 cup
- Kosher salt - ⅓ cup

THE SEASONING

- Garlic, peeled and minced – 3 tablespoons
- Fresh dill, chopped – 1 tablespoon

THE SMOKE

- Preheat, the smoker
- Generously grease the grill rack with nonstick cooking spray

METHOD

1. In a bowl, thoroughly combine the brine ingredients (water, brown sugar, and kosher salt).
2. Place the fish in the brine, and transfer to the fridge for 16 hours.
3. Remove the salmon from the brine, rinse under cold running water, and, using paper towels, pat dry. Allow the fish to rest uncovered on a rack in the fridge for 2-4 hours until a pellicle forms.
4. Season the fish with garlic and fresh dill.
5. Place the salmon on the rack and close the smoker's lid.
6. Smoke the fish for 4 hours, not allowing the smoker to reach more than 180°F (80°C) and no less than 130°F (55°C).
7. Remove the fish from the smoker and serve.
8. Enjoy.

PESTO TOPPED SALMON

(TOTAL COOK TIME 1 HOUR 5 MINUTES)

INGREDIENTS FOR 4 SERVINGS

THE FISH

- 1 large salmon fillet

THE INGREDIENTS

- Olive oil – 1 tablespoon
- Salt and black pepper, as needed, to season
- Basil pesto, store-bought, any brand – 1 cup

THE SMOKE

- Set the smoker to 250°F (120°C)

METHOD

1. Place the salmon fillet on a sheet pan and drizzle with olive oil. Season the fish with salt and black pepper.
2. Spoon the basil pesto over the salmon.
3. Smoke the fish for 60 minutes until it registers an internal temperature of 145°F (65°C).
4. Remove from the smoker and serve.

SALMON WITH BLUEBERRY AND GARLIC CHEESE SAUCE

(TOTAL COOK TIME 45 MINUTES)

INGREDIENTS FOR 4 SERVINGS

THE FISH

- Wild-caught salmon, skin on (2-lb, 0.9-kg)

THE INGREDIENTS

- Worcestershire sauce – 2 tablespoons
- Soy sauce – 2 tablespoons
- Steak seasoning – 2-3 tablespoons

THE BLUEBERRY SAUCE

- Butter – 2 tablespoons
- Olive oil – 1 tablespoon
- 1 medium shallot, minced
- Blueberries (1-lb, 0.45-kg)
- Red wine – ½ cup
- Garlic powder – 1 teaspoon
- Balsamic vinegar – ¼ cup
- Worcestershire sauce – 2 tablespoons
- 4 sprigs of thyme
- Salt and black pepper, as needed, to season
- Cinnamon – 1 teaspoon
- Allspice – 1 teaspoon

THE GARLIC CHEESE SAUCE

- Butter – 2 tablespoons
- 4 garlic cloves, peeled and sliced
- Cream cheese (4-oz, 113.4-gm)
- Buttermilk, divided – ½ cup
- Dijon mustard – 1 tablespoon
- Salt and black pepper, as needed, to season

THE SMOKE

- Set the smoker to 450°F (230°C)
- Choose cherry wood for this recipe

METHOD

1. Liberally coat the fish with Worcestershire sauce and soy sauce. Then season evenly with the steak seasoning to form a thin coating.
2. Lay the salmon skin side facing down on the smoker and close its lid.
3. Smoke the salmon for around 20-30 minutes. The timing will depend on the thickness of the fish. The salmon is ready when it registers an internal temperature of 140°F (60°C). Top the salmon with the blueberry sauce during the final 10 minutes of smoking.
4. For the blueberry sauce. Over moderate heat, in a pan, melt the butter and oil. Then add the shallots and cook for 3-4 minutes, until softened.
5. Add the blueberries and cook for another 3-4 minutes.
6. Pour in the wine, and simmer for approximately 5 minutes.
7. Add the garlic and vinegar and continue to reduce the sauce for 3-4 minutes.
8. Then, add the Worcestershire sauce, thyme sprigs, cinnamon, and allspice. Season to taste with salt and black pepper.
9. Continue to cook the sauce on low to moderate heat for 8-10 minutes, until glossy and thick.
10. Pour the blueberry sauce over the salmon as directed in Step 3.
11. For the garlic cheese sauce, in a pan over moderate heat, melt the butter.
12. Add the garlic to the pan and heat for 5 minutes.
13. Next, stir in the cream cheese until it melts.
14. Add ¼ cup of buttermilk and the mustard and whisk until creamy smooth. You may want to add more buttermilk to achieve your preferred consistency. Season the sauce with salt and black pepper.
15. Drizzle the garlic cheese sauce over the blueberry sauce topped salmon and enjoy.

SMOKED CATFISH

(TOTAL COOK TIME 4 HOURS 30 MINUTES)

INGREDIENTS FOR 4 SERVINGS

THE FISH

- 4 large catfish fillets

THE MARINADE

- Olive oil – ½ cup
- Runny honey – 2 tablespoons
- Cajun seasoning – 2 tablespoons
- Dried thyme – 1 tablespoon
- Coarsely ground sea salt – 1 tablespoon

THE SMOKE

- Set the smoker to 225°F (105°C)

METHOD

1. Add the olive oil to a big bowl. Then add the honey, Cajun seasoning, thyme, and salt, and whisk to incorporate.
2. Add the catfish to the marinade, cover the bowl, and place in the fridge to marinate for a minimum of 4 hours.
3. Remove the fish from the marinade, discarding the marinade.
4. Smoke the fish until it registers an internal temperature of 140°F (60°C).
5. Remove the fish from the smoker and transfer it to a chopping board.
6. Serve and enjoy.

SPICY SMOKED TUNA

(TOTAL COOK TIME 3 HOURS 25 MINUTES)

INGREDIENTS FOR 6 SERVINGS

THE FISH

- 1 Albacore tuna loin

THE MARINADE

- Brown sugar – ¼ cup
- Crushed chili flakes – 1 tablespoon
- Kosher salt – 2 tablespoons
- Zest and fresh juice of 1 lime
- Sriracha sauce – 2 tablespoons
- Soy sauce – 1 tablespoon
- Water – 2 cups

THE SMOKE

- Set the smoker to 140°F (60°C)

METHOD

1. In a bowl, combine the marinade ingredients (brown sugar, crushed chili flakes, kosher salt, lime zest, lime juice, Sriracha sauce, soy sauce, and water).
2. Cut the tuna into segments and add them to the marinade. Set aside to marinate for 20 minutes.
3. Remove the tuna from the marinade, and place in aluminum foil trays.
4. Smoke the tuna for 30-45 minutes.
5. Remove from the smoker and serve.

TUNA STEAKS

(TOTAL COOK TIME 1 HOUR 10 MINUTES)

INGREDIENTS FOR 6 SERVINGS

THE FISH

- 6 tuna steaks

THE MARINADE

- Water - 3 cups
- Kosher salt – ¼ cup
- Brown sugar - ⅓ cup
- Reduced-sodium soy sauce – ¼ cup
- Freshly squeezed juice of 2 limes
- A thumb size piece of ginger, peeled and crushed

THE SMOKE

- Set the smoker to 200°F (90°C)
- Choose your favorite flavor of wood chips

METHOD

1. Add the water, salt, sugar, soy sauce, fresh lime juice, and ginger to a big bowl, and mix well to combine to dissolve the salt and sugar.
2. Add the tuna to ziplock bag, and then pour in the marinade. Transfer the bag to the fridge for 3 hours.
3. Remove the fish from the bag, and rinse under cold running water. Using a kitchen paper towel, pat dry.
4. Lay the fish directly on the smoker's grates and smoke for around 90 minutes or until the fish registers an internal temperature of 140°F (60 °C).
5. Remove the tuna steaks from the smoker and enjoy.

SMOKED CHILEAN SEA BASS

(TOTAL COOK TIME 1 HOUR)

INGREDIENTS FOR 4-6 SERVINGS

THE FISH

- 4 skinless, fresh Chilean sea bass fillets

THE MARINADE

- Canola oil – ¼ cup
- Juice of 1 lemon
- Fresh oregano – 1 tablespoon
- 8 cloves garlic, peeled and crushed
- Fresh thyme – 1 tablespoon
- Blackened rub – 1 teaspoon

THE INGREDIENTS

- Salted butter – ½ cup
- Fish seasoning, as needed

THE SMOKE

- After marinating, when ready to cook, preheat your smoker to 325°F (165°C).
- We recommend apple wood for this recipe

METHOD

1. First, prepare the marinade. In a bowl, combine the oil, lemon juice, oregano, garlic, thyme, and blackened rub. Pour the mixture into a large ziplock bag.
2. Add the sea bass fillets to the ziplock bag and chill for half an hour, turn the fish filets after 15 minutes.
3. Add the butter to a large baking dish. Place the dish in the smoker just long enough for the butter to melt.
4. Pour the marinade into the baking dish.
5. Take the fillets out of the marinade sprinkle each fillet on both sides with fish seasoning and arrange in the baking dish.
6. Cook the fish in the baking dish for half an hour or until the meat registers an internal temperature of 160°F (70°C). Base the fish with the marinade a couple of times during the cooking process.
7. Take the baking dish out of the smoker and remove the fish filets form the marinade and serve!

SMOKED RAINBOW TROUT WITH LEMON DILL SAUCE

(TOTAL COOK TIME 1 HOUR)

INGREDIENTS FOR 4-6 SERVINGS

THE FISH

- 2 boneless fresh rainbow trout fillets, scaled

THE MARINADE

- Fresh ginger, grated – 2 teaspoons
- Maple syrup – ½ cup
- Zest and juice of 1 lemon
- Rice wine vinegar – 2 teaspoons
- Fresh cracked black pepper

THE SAUCE

- Mayonnaise – 1 cup
- Juice and zest of 1 lemon
- Fresh dill, chopped – 1 tablespoon
- Wholegrain mustard – 2 teaspoons
- Black pepper, to taste

THE SMOKE

- After marinating, when ready to cook, preheat your smoker to 220°F (105°C).
- We recommend hickory wood for this recipe

METHOD

1. First, prepare the marinade. Combine all the ingredients (ginger, maple syrup, lemon zest, juice, rice wine vinegar, and black pepper) in a bowl.
2. Add the fish fillets to a large ziplock bag and pour in the marinade. Seal the bag and chill for half an hour.
3. In the meantime, prepare the sauce. Add the mayonnaise, lemon juice, zest, dill, mustard, and black pepper to a bowl and stir to combine. Cover and chill until ready to serve.
4. Take the trout out of the marinade and place it in the smoker. Cook for 20-30 minutes
5. Take the fish out of the smoker and serve with the prepared sauce.

CHERRY-SMOKED CLAMS IN WHITE WINE BUTTER SAUCE

(TOTAL COOK TIME 40 MINUTES)

INGREDIENTS FOR 2 SERVINGS

THE SEAFOOD

- Fresh clams (2-lb, 0.9-kg)

THE BUTTER SAUCE

- Salted butter – ½ cup
- White wine – 1 cup
- 4 sprigs fresh dill, minced

THE SMOKE

- Set the smoker to 275°F (135°C)
- Cherry wood pellets are a good choice for this recipe

METHOD

1. Arrange the clams on your smoker's preheated grate, and smoke for around 30 minutes until the clams open.
2. Add the butter, wine, and dill to a cast-iron pan, and set on your stove over moderate heat. Simmer the butter mixture until it reduces by around 50 percent.
3. Transfer the clams to a dish, and cover them with the butter sauce, setting a little aside for dipping, if required.
4. Serve and enjoy.

SMOKED CRAB CAKES

(TOTAL COOK TIME 2 HOURS 15 MINUTES)

INGREDIENTS FOR 8 SERVINGS

THE SEAFOOD

- Lump crabmeat, picked over (1-lb, 0.5-kg)
- Shrimp, peeled, deveined, and tails removed (4-oz, 100-g)

THE INGREDIENTS

- Milk – 1 cup
- Panko breadcrumbs – 1½ cups
- Salt and black pepper, to season
- Onion, peeled and chopped – ½ cup
- 2 garlic cloves, peeled and smashed
- 2 celery ribs, trimmed and chopped
- Unsalted butter – 2 tablespoons
- Heavy cream – ¼ cup
- Hot pepper sauce – 1 teaspoon
- Freshly squeezed lemon juice – 1 teaspoon
- Dijon mustard – 2 teaspoons
- Old Bay seasoning – ¾ teaspoon

THE SMOKE

- Set the smoker to 250°F (120°C) for indirect cooking

METHOD

1. First, soak the crabmeat in a bowl of milk, and while covered totally, soak it in the fridge for a minimum of 30 minutes.
2. Add the breadcrumbs to a Ziplock bag and crush them using a mallet or rolling pin. Transfer the crushed breadcrumbs to a skillet, and over moderately high heat, toast, while stirring continuously, until golden for around 4 minutes.
3. Transfer the toasted crumbs to a shallow plate and season with ½ teaspoon salt and ½ teaspoon black pepper. Put to one side.
4. Add the onion, garlic, and celery to a food blender and process on pulse 7-8 times.
5. Over moderate heat, preheat a skillet and melt the butter.
6. Then add the pulsed veggies to the skillet and season with ½ teaspoon salt and ½ teaspoon black pepper. Stir the veggies frequently, until tender and most of the moisture evaporated, for around 5 minutes. Transfer the veggies to a big bowl.
7. Press the crabmeat gently against a fine mesh strainer to expel as much milk as possible, but while taking care not to damage any of the crab meat. Discard the milk.
8. Add the shrimp to the blender and pulse 15 times. Next, add the cream and pulse for another 5 times. Scrape down the sides of the blender bowl as necessary.
9. Add the shrimp to the bowl with the cooled veggies, and add the pepper sauce, fresh lemon juice, Dijon mustard, and Old Bay seasoning and stir until combined.
10. Add the crabmeat and fold in until combined.
11. Form the crabmeat mixture into 8 even-size balls.
12. Arrange the crabmeat balls on a parchment-lined baking sheet. Take a spatula and press the balls into patties, around 0.5-in (1-cm). Cover the patties with kitchen wrap, and transfer to the fridge for a minimum of 30 minutes.
13. Finally, press each patty into the breadcrumbs until coated and covered.
14. Smoke the crab cakes for 30 minutes or until they reach an internal temperature of 155°F (65°C).
15. Serve and enjoy.

SMOKED LOBSTER TAILS

(TOTAL COOK TIME 35 MINUTES)

INGREDIENTS FOR 4 SERVINGS

THE SEAFOOD

- 4 medium lobster tails

THE INGREDIENTS

- 1 banana leaf
- Salted butter, softened – 4 tablespoons
- 4 garlic cloves, peeled and crushed
- Sea salt flakes – 1 teaspoon
- Smoked paprika – ⅓ teaspoon
- Freshly squeezed lemon juice
- 1 shallot, sliced
- 1 fresh lemon, sliced
- Parsley, to garnish

THE SMOKE

- Set the smoker to 350°F (175°C)

METHOD

1. First, soak the banana leaf in hot water until softened.
2. Combine the butter, garlic, sea salt, paprika, and fresh lemon juice in a bowl. Combine with a spatula.
3. Using a sharp knife, cut a slit down the middle of each lobster tail and tug gently to pull the meat out and over their shells.
4. Scatter sliced shallots over the lobster tails, and top with lemon slices.
5. Wrap the tails in the banana leaves and arrange them on a baking sheet to carry to your smoker.
6. Lay the lobster directly on the smoker's grill grates.
7. Smoke the lobster for 25 minutes until the meat registers an internal temperature of 140°F (60°C).
8. Remove from the smoker and take the lobster out of the smoker.
9. Enjoy.

SMOKED SHRIMP IN CAJUN GARLIC BUTTER

(TOTAL COOK TIME 45 MINUTES)

INGREDIENTS FOR 8 SERVINGS

THE SEAFOOD

- Shrimp (2-lb, 0.9-kg)

THE INGREDIENTS

- Butter, melted – 1 cup
- 4 garlic cloves, peeled and minced
- Worcestershire sauce – ¼ cup
- 5-6 dashes of Tabasco, to taste
- Freshly squeezed juice of 1 lemon
- Cajun BBQ rub, any brand – 2 teaspoons
- Fresh parsley, chopped – ¼ cup
- Red pepper flakes, to garnish

THE SMOKE

- Set the smoker to 250°F (120°C) for indirect cooking
- Add your choice of wood pellets

METHOD

1. Over moderately high heat, place a cast iron skillet on the smoker's burner.
2. Melt the butter in the skillet and then remove it from the heat sources and place it on a cool burner.
3. Add the garlic to the butter, and combine with the Worcestershire sauce, Tabasco (to taste), fresh lemon juice, and Cajun seasoning.
4. Add the shrimp to the garlic butter mixture and turn them over until they are coated fully. Then place the shrimp in the skillet, so they lay flat to ensure an even cook. Cook the shrimp for 30-45 minutes. The timings will depend on the size of the shrimp, but they are good to go when they register an internal temperature of 145°F (60°C) and are no longer translucent.
5. Garnish the shrimp with parsley and red pepper flakes and enjoy.

SMOKED OYSTERS WITH COMPOUND BACON- BUTTER

(TOTAL COOK TIME 1 HOUR 5 MINUTES)

INGREDIENTS FOR 4 SERVINGS

THE SEAFOOD

- 24 fresh whole oysters, shucked

THE INGREDIENTS

- 2 rashers of smoked bacon, cut in half
- Butter, room temperature – ½ cup
- 2 garlic cloves, peeled and minced
- Fresh parsley, minced – 1 tablespoon
- 4 lemon wedges, to serve

THE SMOKE

- Add a combination of white wine and water to the water bowl
- Add applewood wood chips to the tray
- Preheat the smoker to 225°F (107°C) with the top vent open and the door closed

METHOD

1. Over moderate to high heat, heat a frying pan or skillet.
2. Add 4 bacon halves to the pan and cook until crisp. Remove the bacon from the pan and place on a plate lined with kitchen paper to drain.
3. Add the butter to a bowl.
4. Crumble the crisp bacon and add it to the butter, followed by the garlic.
5. With a fork, stir in the parsley.
6. Place the bacon butter on a piece of kitchen wrap and form into a log-shape approximately 1-ins (2.5-cms) in diameter.
7. Roll the butter in the wrap tightly and from into a cylindrical-shape. Twist the ends tightly.
8. Transfer the compound butter to the freezer until cold enough to slice into coins.
9. Place the shucked oysters on a sheet tray, taking care not to overcrowd the oysters or spill any of their liquid.
10. Remove the butter from the freezer.
11. Unwrap the butter and into coins 0.25-ins (0.65-cms) thick.
12. Place a butter coin on top of each of the oysters.
13. Transfer the sheet tray(s) to the smoker and smoke for half an hour until they are smoky and their edges curled. If they are not cooked to this level, return to the smoker and smoke in 15-minute intervals. Take care, though, not to over-smoke and dry the oysters out.
14. Serve with wedges of fresh lemon.

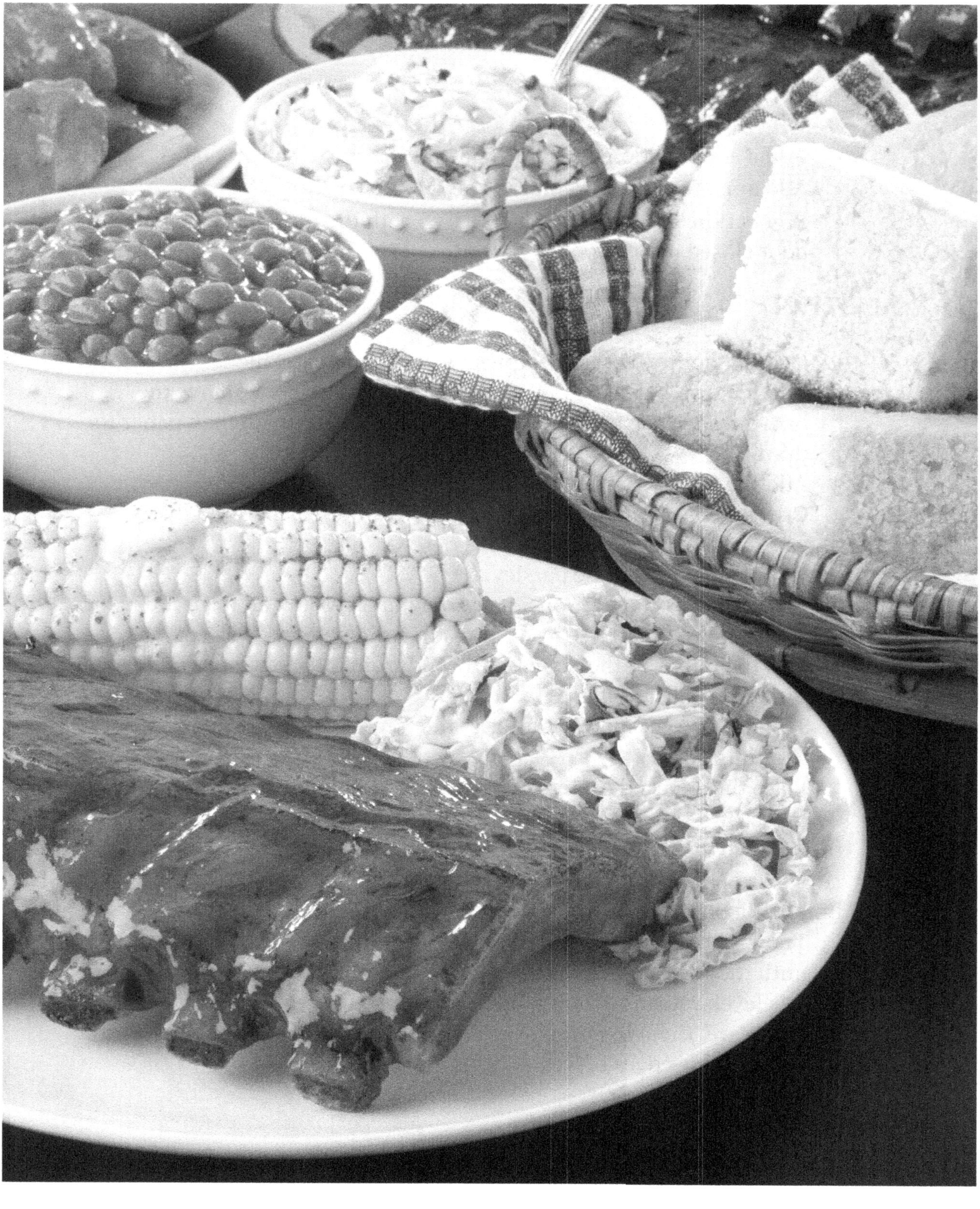

CHAPTER 7
BURGERS, SAUSAGES, AND MORE

SMOKED LAMB BURGERS - 128
GARDEN HERB SEASONED SMOKED TURKEY SAUSAGES - 130
CHIPOTLE TURKEY BURGERS - 132
HOMEMADE SALSA - 134
SMOKED CORNBREAD - 136
SMOKED MAC' N CHEESE - 138
WILD BOAR SAUSAGES - 140
SMOKED BEEF HEART - 142
CHEESY SMOKED PIZZA WITH SAUSAGE AND PEPPERONI - 144

SMOKED LAMB BURGERS

(TOTAL COOK TIME 1 HOUR)

INGREDIENTS FOR 4 SERVINGS

THE MEAT

- Ground lamb (1.5-lbs, 0.7-kgs)

THE INGREDIENTS

- Sea salt – 2 teaspoons
- Freshly ground black pepper – 2 teaspoons
- 4 slices of Havarti cheese
- 4 brioche burger buns
- 2 large lettuce leaves

THE SMOKE

- When you are ready to start cooking, preheat the smoker to 250°F (120°C)
- Cherry or applewood wood chips are a great choice for this recipe

METHOD

1. In a bowl, combine the lamb with the salt and black pepper.
2. Divide the mixture into quarters, and shape the mixture into patties.
3. Put the patties in the smoker and cook until the lamb registers an internal temperature of 150°F (65 °C). Add the cheese. The smoking time is approximately 45 minutes. Continue to smoke for an additional 15 minutes.
4. Serve the burgers inside the brioche burger buns and top with a lettuce leaf.

GARDEN HERB SEASONED SMOKED TURKEY SAUSAGES

(TOTAL COOK TIME 2 HOURS 35 MINUTES)

INGREDIENTS FOR 4-6 SERVINGS

THE MEAT

- Ground turkey (3-lbs, 1.4-kgs)

THE INGREDIENTS

- ½ yellow onion, peeled and finely diced
- Fresh parsley, finely chopped – 3 tablespoons
- Fresh sage, finely chopped – 3 tablespoons
- Fresh rosemary, finely chopped – 3 tablespoons
- Fresh thyme, finely chopped – 3 tablespoons
- Hog casing, as needed, soaked
- Salt – 3 teaspoons
- Freshly ground black pepper – 1 teaspoon

THE SMOKE

- Preheat your smoker to 225°F (110°C)
- Sage wood chips are a good choice for this recipe

METHOD

1. In a mixing bowl, combine the ground turkey with the onion, parsley, sage, rosemary, and thyme.
2. Soak the hog casing for 30 minutes in cold water.
3. Remove the casing from the cold water and flush out with fresh cold water.
4. Stuff the hog casing with the turkey-garden herb mixture and twist the links to encase.
5. Hand the stuffed sausages, and smoke for 2-4 hours, or until they register an internal temperature of 165°F (75°C).

CHIPOTLE TURKEY BURGERS

(TOTAL COOK TIME 55 MINUTES)

INGREDIENTS FOR 8 SERVINGS

THE MEAT

- Ground turkey (2-lbs, 0.9-kgs)

THE INGREDIENTS

- Onion, peeled, finely chopped – ½ cup
- Fresh cilantro, chopped – 3 tablespoons
- 2 chipotle chilies in adobo sauce
- Garlic powder – 2 teaspoons
- Onion powder – 2 teaspoon
- Beef rub, of choice – 3 tablespoons
- 8 Pepper Jack cheese slices
- 8 sesame seed hamburger buns, split

THE SMOKE

- With the lid closed, preheat your smoker to 375°F (190°C) for 15-20 minutes
- Choose your favorite wood chips for this recipe

METHOD

1. In a large bowl, combine the ground turkey with the onions, cilantro, chipotle chilies, garlic powder, onion powder, and beef rub. Using clean hands, form the mixture into 8 even size patties.
2. Cook the burgers in the preheated smoker for approximately 45 minutes or until the meat registers an internal temperature of 165°F (75°C).
3. Just before you remove the burgers from the smoker, top each one with a slice of cheese and serve inside a hamburger bun.

HOMEMADE SALSA

(TOTAL COOK TIME 35 MINUTES)

INGREDIENTS FOR 8 SERVINGS

THE INGREDIENTS

- 2 large beefsteak tomatoes, sliced into quarters
- ½ large onion, peeled and sliced into quarters
- 1 jalapeno pepper, halved
- Olive oil – 2 teaspoons
- Garlic, peeled and minced – 2 teaspoons
- Fresh cilantro – ¼ cup
- Salt and black pepper, to season

THE SMOKE

- Set the smoker to 225°F (105°C) for indirect heat

METHOD

1. Place the tomatoes, onion, and jalapeno on a platter and drizzle with oil. Then season with salt and black pepper.
2. Arrange the tomato, onion, and jalapenos on the grates of the preheated smoker and smoke for 1 hour 30 minutes.
3. Remove the veggies from the smoker and add them to a food blender along with the garlic and cilantro. Process to a chunky puree, and season with salt and pepper.
4. Serve the salsa as a side.

SMOKED CORNBREAD

(TOTAL COOK TIME 35 MINUTES)

INGREDIENTS FOR 8 SERVINGS

THE INGREDIENTS

- Flour – 1 cup
- Cornmeal – 1⅓ cups
- Baking powder – 2 teaspoons
- Bicarbonate of soda – ½ teaspoon
- Salt – 1 teaspoon
- 1 egg
- Butter, melted – ⅓ cup + more to serve
- Runny honey – ½ cup + more to serve
- Milk – 1 cup
- Cheddar cheese, shredded – ½ cup

THE SMOKE

- Set the smoker to 400°F (200°C) for indirect heat

METHOD

1. In a big bowl, combine the flour, cornmeal, baking powder, bicarb, and salt and whisk to incorporate.
2. Make a well-shape in the middle of the dry ingredients, and add the egg, butter, honey, and milk. Whisk to create a thick batter.
3. Then fold in the shredded cheese.
4. Spoon the batter into a seasoned 9-in (23-cm) cast iron pan.
5. Place the pan on the smoker and smoke until springy to the touch and golden for 20-25 minutes.
6. Remove from the smoker and allow to cool before slicing and serving with more honey and butter.

SMOKED MAC' N CHEESE

(TOTAL COOK TIME 1 HOUR 20 MINUTES)

INGREDIENTS FOR 8 SERVINGS

THE INGREDIENTS

- Elbow macaroni, cooked according to package directions (1-lb, 0.5-gm)
- Butter – ½ cup
- Cream cheese (4-oz, 110-gm)
- Flour – 4 tablespoons
- Mustard powder – 1 tablespoon
- Half and half – 2 cups
- Cheddar cheese, grated – 3 cups
- Gouda, grated – 1½ cups

THE BREADCRUMB TOPPING

- Butter, melted – ¼ cup
- Sweet rub, any brand, of choice – 2 tablespoons
- Panko breadcrumbs – 1 cup

THE SMOKE

- Set the smoker to 225°F (105°C) for indirect heat
- Use cherry or applewood chips for this recipe

METHOD

1. Bring a large pot of salted water to a boil. Cook the pasta in the water until al dente.
2. Over moderate heat, heat a 12-in (30-cm) iron skillet.
3. In the skillet, melt ½ cup of butter and whisk in the cream cheese until silky smooth. Next, whisk in the flour, mustard powder, and half and half until thickened.
4. Then, whisk in the grated Cheddar and Gouda, stirring until it melts. Turn the heat off and add the macaroni. Gently stir until the macaroni is coated in the cheesy sauce.
5. In a small bowl, combine the melted butter with the sweet rub and breadcrumbs. Scatter the mixture over the surface of the Mac n Cheese.
6. Place the skillet in the smoker, close its lid, and smoke for 60 minutes.
7. Serve and enjoy.

WILD BOAR SAUSAGES

(TOTAL COOK TIME 11 HOURS)

INGREDIENTS FOR 4-6 SERVINGS

THE MEAT

- Ground wild boar (1-lb, 0.5-kgs)

THE INGREDIENTS

- Quick salt tender – 1½ teaspoons
- Kosher salt – 1 tablespoon
- Mustard seeds _ ½ teaspoon
- Black pepper – ½ teaspoon
- Garlic powder– ½ teaspoon

THE SMOKE

- Preheat your smoker for 15 minutes to 225°F (105°C)

METHOD

1. In a bowl, combine the quick salt tender, kosher salt, mustard seeds, black pepper, and garlic powder and mix lightly. Allow the mixture to rest in the refrigerator for 8 hours.
2. Form the meat into a log-shape and wrap in plastic wrap. Twist the ends of the wrap. Using your finger, smooth out the log. Slowly unwrap, to maintain its even shape.
3. Transfer to the smoker and cook for 3-4 hours.
4. Remove from the smoker and set aside to cool for 1 hour at room temperature.
5. Unwrap, and store in the fridge until needed.

SMOKED BEEF HEART

(TOTAL COOK TIME 9 HOURS)

INGREDIENTS FOR 6 SERVINGS

THE MEAT

- 1 beef heart (2-lb, 0.9-kg)

THE INGREDIENTS

- Olive oil, as needed
- Beef rub, as needed
- Soy sauce – ¼ cup
- Worcestershire sauce - ½ cup
- Garlic, peeled and minced
- Fresh rosemary stems
- Fresh thyme stems
- Duck fat in spray bottle, to spritz

THE SMOKE

- Preheat, the smoker to 180°F (80°C)
- Choose oak wood chips for this recipe

METHOD

1. Prepare the heart by first slicing it down the middle. Next, open and remove the webbing. Finally, trim off some surface fat.
2. Rub oil all over the meat, followed by the rub.
3. Transfer the meat to a large ziplock bag.
4. In a bowl, combine the soy sauce with Worcestershire sauce, garlic, rosemary, and thyme. Add the mixture to the ziplock bag, and place in the fridge overnight.
5. Smoke the meat until it registers an internal temperature of 120°F (50°C).
6. Heat your grill to hot.
7. Spray the heart with duck fat and transfer to the grill, searing for 2-3 minutes, on each side.
8. Loosely tent the meat in foil, and set aside for 10 minutes before slicing.
9. Serve.

CHEESY SMOKED PIZZA WITH SAUSAGE AND PEPPERONI

(TOTAL COOK TIME 25 MINUTES)

INGREDIENTS FOR 4 SERVINGS

THE MEAT

- Pork sausage, cooked (5-oz, 150-gm)

THE PIZZA

- Olive oil – 1 tablespoon
- 1 pizza dough, store-bought
- Pizza sauce, store-bought – ½ cup
- Mozzarella cheese, shredded – 1 cup
- 25 slices pepperoni

THE SMOKE

- Set the smoker to 450°F (230°C)
- Place a pizza stone inside the smoker to preheat

METHOD

1. Spread the olive oil over the store-bought pizza crust.
2. Spread the pizza sauce over the surface of the crust.
3. Top with mozzarella cheese.
4. Arrange the pork sausage over the cheese, followed by the slices of pepperoni over the top of the pizza.
5. Smoke the pizza on the preheated pizza stone for 12-16 minutes until the cheese melts, and the crust is crisp.
6. Remove from the smoker and enjoy.

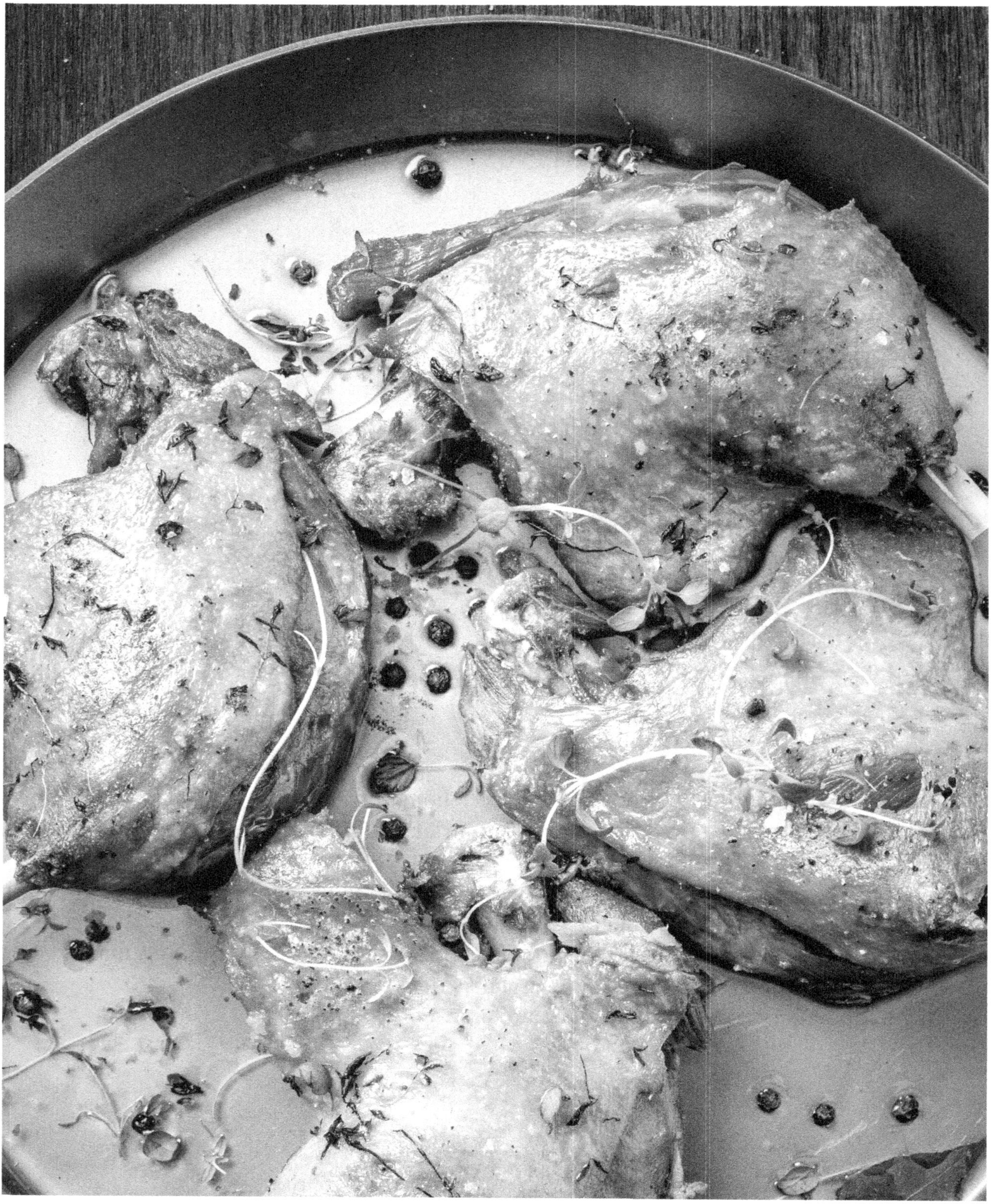

CHAPTER 8
GAME MEATS

BRAISED SWAN LEGS – 149
GOOSE BRACIOLE – 151
CRUSTED SMOKED RABBIT – 153
COLD SMOKED DUCK CARPACCIO – 155
SMOKED GOOSE TACOS – 157
BISON BRISKET – 160
RASPBERRY-GLAZED ELK STEAKS – 162
HICKORY SMOKED VENISON ROAST – 164
SPICY COFFEE RUBBED SMOKED VENISON BRISKET – 166
BBQ SMOKED VENISON RIBS – 168

CUTS OF DUCK

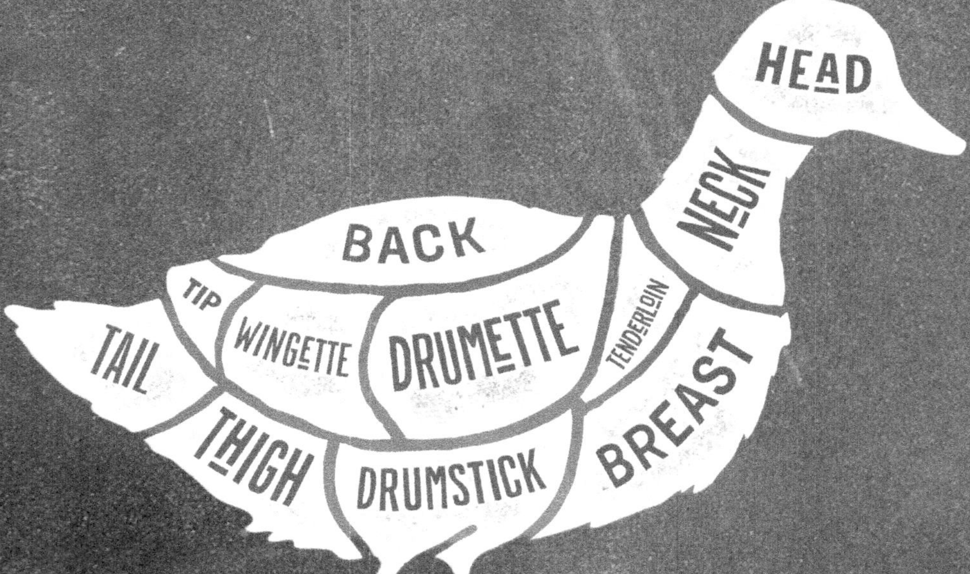
HEAD
NECK
BACK
TIP
WINGETTE
DRUMETTE
TENDERLOIN
TAIL
THIGH
DRUMSTICK
BREAST

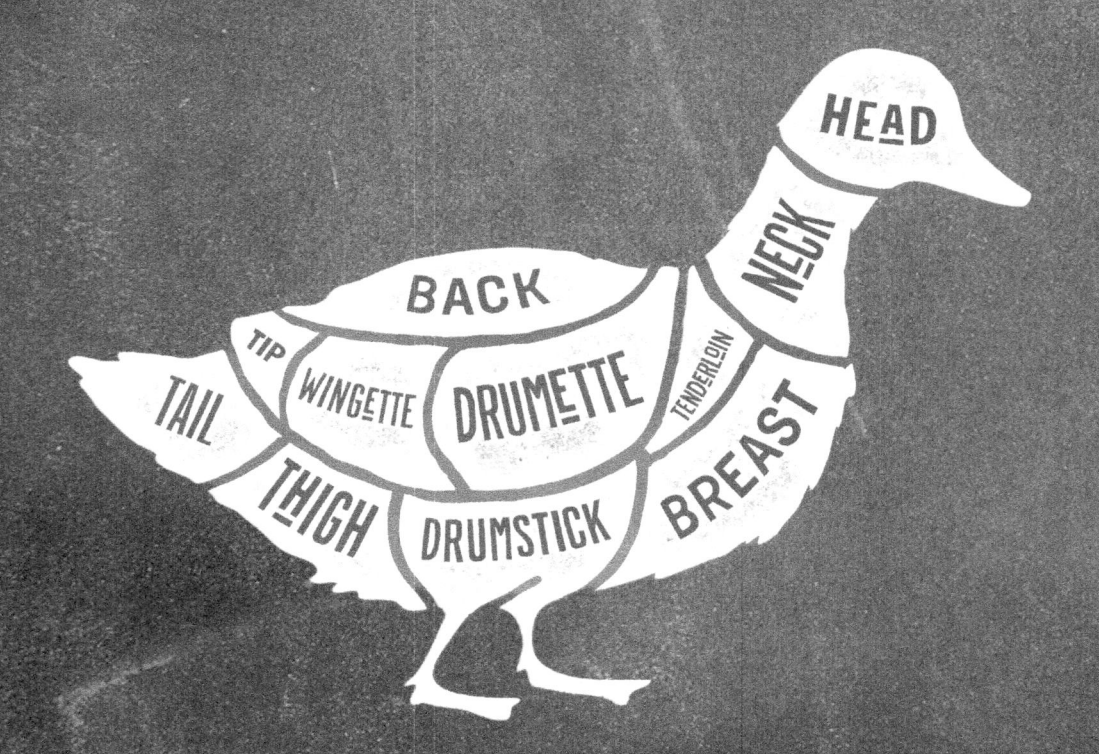

BRAISED SWAN LEGS

(TOTAL COOK TIME 4 HOURS 30 MINUTES)

INGREDIENTS FOR 4 SERVINGS

THE MEAT

- 2 swan legs

THE INGREDIENTS

- Salt and black pepper, to season
- 4 slices bacon, cut into 2-in (5-cm) pieces
- Unsalted butter – 2 tablespoons
- Shallots, coarsely chopped – 1½ cups
- 6 garlic cloves
- 2 tomatoes, quartered and crushed
- Red wine – ½ cup
- 2 bay leaves

THE SMOKE

- Set the smoker to 225°F (105°C) with the lid closed for 15 minutes

METHOD

1. Season the swan legs with salt and black pepper.
2. Over moderate heat, heat a large Dutch oven.
3. Add the bacon pieces to the Dutch oven and cook until browned lightly. Then add the butter, shallots, whole garlic, and seasoned swan legs to the Dutch oven, and brown the legs on both sides.
4. Next, stir in the crushed tomatoes, red wine, and bay leaves. Remove the Dutch oven from the heat.
5. Place the Dutch oven, uncovered, on the smoker. Close the smoker's lid and heavy smoke for 60 minutes. Turn the heavy smoke off and cover the Dutch oven with its lid. Continue to cook the swan legs for 2 hours before increasing the smoker temperature to 325°F (165°C) and cook for another 60 minutes.
6. Remove from the smoker and allow to rest for 15 minutes.
7. Serve the swan legs and enjoy.

GOOSE BRACIOLE

(TOTAL COOK TIME 4 HOURS 45 MINUTES)

INGREDIENTS FOR 4 SERVINGS

THE MEAT

- 2 boneless, skinless goose breasts

THE INGREDIENTS

- Granulated garlic powder – 1 teaspoon
- Basil pesto, store-bought – ½ cup
- 4 slices prosciutto
- 4 bacon slices
- Olive oil – 1 tablespoon

THE SMOKE

- Set the smoker to 375°F (190°C) with the lid closed for 15 minutes

METHOD

1. Place the goose breasts on a chopping board. Take a knife, hold it horizontally to the board, then make a cut along the middle side and cut all the way through to yield 4 pieces. Pound the breast portions to flatten.
2. Next, season the flattened goose with granulated garlic powder. Spread a thin layer of basil pesto over the breasts and top each one with a slice of prosciutto.
3. Beginning on one side, roll the goose up and then wrap it with a slice of bacon. Secure the bacon using kitchen twine and drizzle with olive oil. Set aside and continue with the remaining goose pieces.
4. Place the wrapped goose on the smoker's grill grates, close the smoker's lid, and cook for 10 minutes.
5. Flip the goose oven and cook for another 10 minutes.
6. Remove the heat and put aside to rest for 19 minutes.
7. Remove the kitchen twine, slice, serve and enjoy.

CRUSTED SMOKED RABBIT

(TOTAL COOK TIME 5 HOURS 25 MINUTES)

INGREDIENTS FOR 4 SERVINGS

THE MEAT

- 1 whole rabbit (3-lbs, 1.4-kgs)

THE DRY RUB

- Paprika – ¼ cup
- Garlic powder – 3 tablespoons
- Sea salt – 3 tablespoons
- Onion powder – 1½ tablespoons
- Freshly ground black pepper – 2 ½ tablespoons
- Cayenne pepper – 2 teaspoons
- Brown sugar – 1½ teaspoons
- Dried mustard powder – 1 teaspoon

THE SMOKE

- Preheat, the smoker to 240°F (115°C)
- Hickory wood chips are a good choice for this recipe
- Add water to the water bowl

METHOD

1. In a bowl, combine the paprika, garlic powder, salt, onion powder, black pepper, cayenne, brown sugar, and mustard.
2. Put the rabbit in a baking dish.
3. Pack the dry rub all around the rabbit.
4. Lay a piece of kitchen wrap on a clean work surface, and place the rabbit in the center of the wrap. Seal the rabbit tightly in the wrap. Transfer to a baking dish and place in the fridge for a minimum of 2 hours.
5. Take the wrapped rabbit out of the fridge and allow to come to room temperature before smoking.
6. Put the whole rabbit on the smoker rack and place in the smoke for 90 minutes. Turn the rabbit over; add more wood chips and water, as necessary. Continue to smoke the rabbit for an additional 90 minutes before checking the internal temperature of the meat is 165°F (75°C).
7. Take the rabbit out of the smoker and place it on a chopping board.
8. Tent with aluminum foil and set aside to rest for 15 minutes.
9. Carve the rabbit into portions (thighs, legs, and split saddles).
10. Serve and enjoy.

COLD SMOKED DUCK CARPACCIO

(TOTAL COOK TIME 24 HOURS 45 MINUTES)

INGREDIENTS FOR 4 SERVINGS

THE MEAT

- 1 skin-on duck breast

THE INGREDIENTS

- Rock sea salt – 1 cup
- Sugar – 1 cup
- Freshly squeezed juice of ½ fresh lime
- White truffle oil – 1 tablespoon
- Mixed greens, to serve
- Pinch of sea salt

THE SMOKE

- Add 3 lit charcoal briquettes to the middle of the firebox followed by 2 cups of cherry, maple or apple wood chips
- Open the intake damper and chimney by ½ -in (1.25-cms)
- To cold smoke, you will need to keep the temperature under 110°F (45°C), so smoke early in the morning or at night time. If the outside temperature is above 90°F (30°C), you will need to place a large size ice-filled aluminum drip pan between the firebox and the meat; this will help to maintain a low temperature

METHOD

1. In a bowl, combine the rock salt with the sugar.
2. Add half of the salt-sugar mixture to a pan.
3. Place the duck breast on top of the mixture in the pan. Cover the duck with the remaining half of the salt-sugar.
4. Using plastic kitchen wrap, cover the pan. Place a heavy pan on top of the meat and place it in the fridge for 24 hours.
5. The next day, under cold running water, rinse the duck breast. Using kitchen paper towels, pat the duck dry.
6. Add the breast to the cold smoker for 20-60 minutes, until you achieve your desired level of doneness.
7. Slice and serve with freshly squeezed lime juice, a drizzle of truffle oil, and mixed greens. Season with sea salt and serve.

SMOKED GOOSE TACOS

(TOTAL COOK TIME 28 HOURS 25 MINUTES)

INGREDIENTS FOR 6-8 SERVINGS

THE MEAT

- 2 whole Specklebelly geese, plucked and cleaned

THE BRINE

- Kosher salt – ½ cup
- Water – 8 cups

THE DRY RUB

- Dark brown sugar – 2 tablespoons
- Paprika – 2 teaspoons
- Allspice – 1 teaspoon
- White pepper – 1 teaspoon
- Chinese 5 spice powder – ½ teaspoon

THE CILANTRO SAUCE

- Cilantro, coarsely chopped – 2 cups
- 1 garlic clove, peeled and chopped
- Vinegar – 1 tablespoon
- Olive oil – ½ cup

THE INGREDIENTS

- Corn tortillas, warmed, as needed
- Cabbage slaw, as needed, shredded
- 4 green apples, cored and thinly sliced

THE SMOKE

- Set the smoker to 250°F (120°C)

METHOD

1. Place the cleaned geese in a plastic dish.
2. For the brine: In a bowl, combine the water with the salt and pour over the birds, making sure they are submerged. Cover the dish and transfer to the fridge for 24 hours.
3. Remove the geese from the brine and rinse well until cold running water. Place on a rack set over a baking sheet and allow to air dry for 2 hours.
4. For the dry rub, in a bowl, combine the dark brown sugar with the paprika, allspice, white pepper, and Chinese 5 spice powder. Rub the mixture all over the surface and interior of the geese.
5. For the sauce, in a food blender, process the cilantro, garlic clove, vinegar, and oil, until smooth. Scrape down the sides of the blender as needed and set aside until needed.
6. Place the birds on the grill grates and smoker for 2 hours. The meat is ready when it registers an internal temperature of 150°F (65°C). Remove the geese and cover loosely with foil. Allow to rest for around half an hour before slicing.
7. Add the slices of meat to corn tortillas, and top with shredded slaw, sliced green apples, and cilantro sauce.

BISON BRISKET

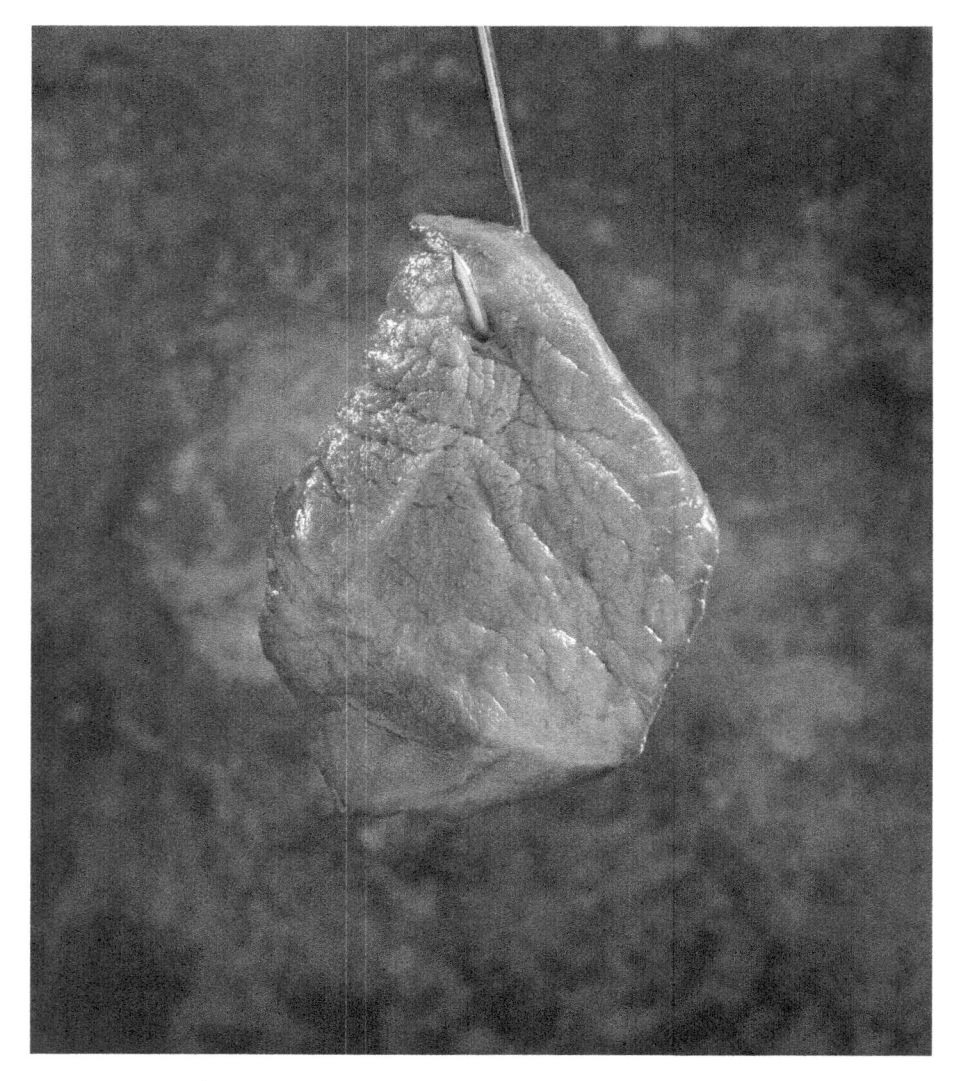

(TOTAL COOK TIME 2 ½ DAYS)

INGREDIENTS FOR 4 SERVINGS

THE MEAT

- Bison brisket (3-lb, 1.5-kg)

THE INGREDIENTS

- Kosher salt and black pepper, as needed, to season
- Dark red ale, any brand, quantity as needed
- BBQ sauce, any brand, quantity as needed
- Chicken stock, quantity as needed
- Olive oil, as needed

THE SMOKE

- Set the smoker to 200°F (95°C) for indirect heat

METHOD

1. Generously season the meat on all sides with salt and black pepper. Transfer to the fridge for 48 hours before smoking.
2. Once you are ready to begin smoking, lay the meat on the smoker's rack and smoke for 2 hours.
3. When 2 hours have elapsed, the meat should have an internal temperature of around 120°F (50°C). Then, coat the meat all over with oil. Smoke for another 30 minutes.
4. Drizzle ale and BBQ sauce over the meat, followed by chicken stock.
5. With pink butcher paper, wrap the bison brisket.
6. Place the meat in a foil tray and return to the smoker. You will need to check every 60 minutes to ensure enough liquid exists to keep the meat moist.
7. After 4½ hours, increase the smoker's temperature to 240°F (110°C). Continue checking on the meat's smoking process every 60 minutes, adding more liquid as needed.
8. When 12-14 hours have elapsed, and the meat has reached an internal temperature of around 200°F (95°C), remove from the smoker. Cover the tray and meat wrapped tightly with foil and allow to cool for 60 minutes before slicing.
9. Enjoy.

RASPBERRY-GLAZED ELK STEAKS

(TOTAL COOK TIME 9 HOURS 15 MINUTES)

INGREDIENTS FOR 4 SERVINGS

THE MEAT

- 3 large elk steaks
- Montreal steak seasoning – 3 tablespoons

THE MARINADE

- Dijon mustard – ½ cup
- Balsamic vinegar – ½ cup
- 2 garlic cloves, peeled and minced
- 1 sprig of rosemary, chopped
- Salt – 1 teaspoon
- Black pepper – ½ teaspoon

THE GLAZE

- Fresh raspberries, mashed – 1/8 cup
- Fresh huckleberries, mashed – 1/8 cup
- Brown sugar – ¼ cup
- Cornstarch – 1 tablespoon
- Water – ¼ cup

THE SMOKE

- Set the smoker to 275°F (135°C) for indirect heat

METHOD

1. Place the elk steaks in a ziplock bag.
2. Add the marinade ingredients (mustard, balsamic vinegar, garlic, rosemary sprig, salt, and black pepper) to the bag and transfer to the fridge to chill overnight.
3. Take the elk steaks out of the ziplock bag and discard the marinade.
4. Rub the elk steaks all over with steak seasoning.
5. Lay the steaks on the smoker's grate and smoke for 60 minutes until the meat registers an internal temperature of 140°F (60°C).
6. In the meantime, heat a small pan over moderately high heat and add the raspberries, huckleberries, brown sugar, and a splash of water. Bring the mixture to a boil.
7. Then pour the mixture through a strainer and into a glass bowl. Discard the seeds and pour the mixture back into the small pan.
8. In a small bowl, whisk the cornstarch with the water. Pour the slurry into the sauce, stirring until thickened.
9. Place the smoked elk steaks on a chopping board and tent with aluminum foil. Allow to rest for 5 minutes before slicing.
10. Drizzle the sauce over the meat and enjoy.

HICKORY SMOKED VENISON ROAST

(TOTAL COOK TIME 2 HOURS 20 MINUTES)

INGREDIENTS FOR 4 SERVINGS

THE MEAT

- Venison roast (2-lb, 0.9-kg)
- Olive oil – 2 tablespoons

THE RUB

- Kosher salt – ¼ teaspoon
- Smoked paprika – 2 tablespoons
- Garlic powder – 2 tablespoons
- Ground black pepper – 2 tablespoons
- Onion powder – 2 tablespoons
- Cilantro – 1 tablespoon
- Cumin – 1 tablespoon
- Cayenne pepper – 1 tablespoon

THE SMOKE

- Add hickory wood chips to the wood tray
- Set the smoker to 225°F (105°C)
- Place a pan under the grates to catch any drippings and retain moisture during the smoking process

METHOD

1. In a small bowl, combine the salt, smoked paprika, garlic powder, ground black pepper, onion powder, cilantro, cumin, and cayenne pepper. Using a fork, crush any lumps.
2. Apply a fine layer of oil to the surface of the roast, covering evenly.
3. Apply the rub over the meat, covering all sides, and working into any surface crevices.
4. When the smoker is at the desired temperature, place the meat on the grates.
5. Smoke the venison until it registers an internal temperature of 140°F (60°C).
6. When the venison is ready, remove it from the smoker. Loosely tent in foil and set aside to rest for 10 minutes.
7. Slice the meat and serve.

SPICY COFFEE RUBBED SMOKED VENISON BRISKET

(TOTAL COOK TIME 14 HOURS 15 MINUTES)

INGREDIENTS FOR 2 SERVINGS

THE MEAT

- Venison brisket, patted dry (1-lb, 0.9-kg)

THE RUB

- Coarsely ground coffee – 2 tablespoons
- Chili powder – 2 tablespoons
- Coconut sugar – 2 tablespoons
- Salt – 1 teaspoon
- Cumin – 1 teaspoon
- Cayenne pepper, to taste – ½ - 1 teaspoon
- Red pepper flakes, to taste – ½ - 1 teaspoon

THE SMOKE

- Set the smoker to 225°F (105°C)
- Add your choice of wood chips to the wood tray

METHOD

1. In a small bowl, whisk the rub ingredients (ground coffee, chili powder, coconut sugar, salt, cumin, cayenne pepper, and red pepper flakes).
2. Using around half of the rub (3 tablespoons), work the rub into the meat to cover entirely and on both sides.
3. Then wrap the venison brisket tightly in kitchen wrap, and transfer to the fridge for 12-24 hours.
4. Remove the meat from the fridge and allow it to stand until room temperature.
5. When the smoker is at the correct temperature, place the meat directly in the smoker. Smoke for approximately 2 hours, or until the venison registers an internal temperature of 150°F (65°C).
6. Let the venison rest for around 20 minutes before slicing and serving.

BBQ SMOKED VENISON RIBS

(TOTAL COOK TIME 10 HOURS 30 MINUTES)

INGREDIENTS FOR 2-4 SERVINGS

THE MEAT

- 1 rack venison spare ribs, membrane removed, visible fat trimmed

THE BRINE

- Water – 16 cups
- Kosher salt – ½ cup
- Brown sugar – 1 cup
- Soy sauce – 1 cup
- Molasses – 1 cup
- Ground black pepper – 1 tablespoon
- Rosemary – 1 tablespoon
- Worcestershire sauce – ¼ cup

THE BBQ RUB

- Kosher salt – ¼ teaspoon
- Smoked paprika – 2 tablespoons
- Garlic powder – 2 tablespoons
- Ground black pepper – 2 tablespoons
- Onion powder – 2 tablespoons
- Cumin – 1 tablespoon
- Cilantro – 1 tablespoon
- Cayenne pepper – 1 tablespoon

THE SMOKE

- Set the smoker to 225°F (105°C)
- Add your choice of wood chips to the wood tray

METHOD

1. In a bucket, prepare the brine by combining the following ingredients (kosher salt, smoked paprika, garlic powder, ground black pepper, onion powder, cumin, cilantro, and cayenne pepper).
2. Lower the ribs into the bucket of brine to submerge. Cover with a lid and transfer to the fridge overnight.
3. Take the ribs out of the brine and, with kitchen paper, pat dry. Leave the ribs on a drying rack for half an hour.
4. Set the smoker for indirect smoking and heat to 225°F (105°C).
5. When the smoker is at the correct heat, place the ribs on the grates. Close the smoker lid and cook until tender and pulling away from the bones. This process will take 1½ -2 hours.
6. Enjoy.

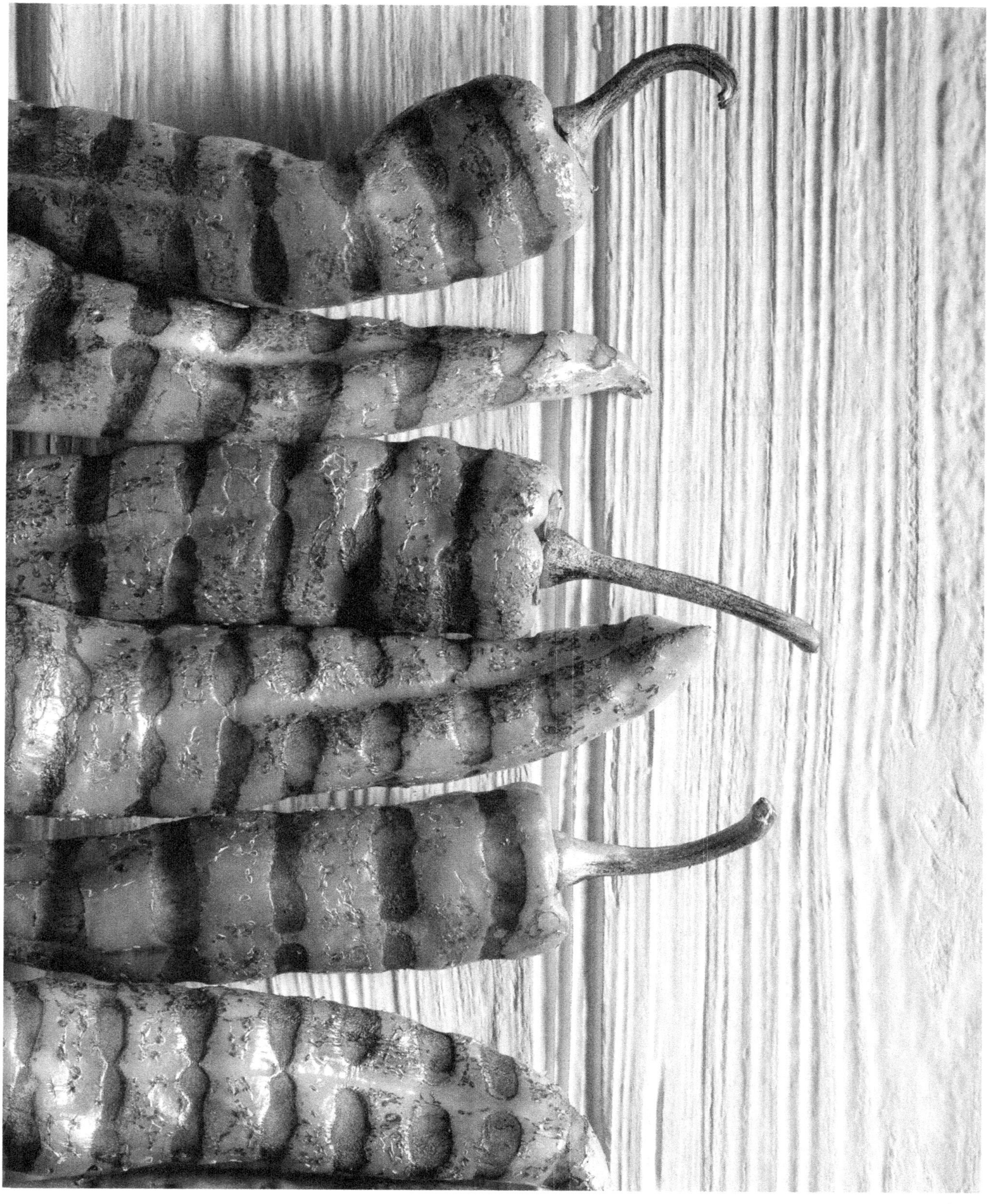

CHAPTER 9
VEGGIES

DOUBLE SMOKED ARTICHOKE DIP - 172
SMOKED CAULIFLOWER - 174
SMOKED JALAPENOS - 176
SMOKED NEW POTATO AND EGG SALAD - 178
BUTTER SMOKED CABBAGE - 180

DOUBLE SMOKED ARTICHOKE DIP

(TOTAL COOK TIME 4 HOURS 15 MINUTES)

INGREDIENTS FOR 8 SERVINGS

THE INGREDIENTS

- 2 whole garlic cloves, peeled
- Olive oil – 1 tablespoon
- Cream cheese (8-oz, 200-gm)
- Sour cream – ½ cup
- Mayonnaise – ½ cup
- 1 can artichoke hearts, chopped (14-oz, 400-gm)
- Salt, black pepper, and granulated garlic seasoning – 1 teaspoon
- Mozzarella cheese – 2 cups
- Parmesan cheese, shredded – 1 cup

THE SMOKE

- Set the smoker to 180°F (82°C)

METHOD

1. Brush the whole garlic cloves with oil and place on a baking sheet and smoke for 2 hours.
2. Remove the garlic cloves from the smoker and increase its temperature to 275°F (135°C).
3. In a bowl, combine the cream cheese with the roasted garlic, sour cream, mayonnaise, artichokes, salt, black pepper, granulated garlic, and mozzarella. Mix well until incorporated and transfer to an 8-in (20-cm) square heat-safe baking dish. Scatter shredded Parmesan over the top.
4. Return to the smoker and bake for 60 minutes.
5. Serve hot with pita, veggies, or crackers.

SMOKED CAULIFLOWER

(TOTAL COOK TIME 4 HOURS 15 MINUTES)

INGREDIENTS FOR 8 SERVINGS

THE INGREDIENTS

- Fresh cauliflower florets – 9 cups
- Olive oil – 2 tablespoons
- Salt – 1 teaspoon
- Garlic powder – 1 teaspoon
- Dijon mustard – ¼ cup
- Maple syrup – 1-2 tablespoons
- Fresh parsley, minced – 2 tablespoons

THE SMOKE

- Set the smoker to 250°F (120°C)
- Use hickory or apple wood chips for this recipe

METHOD

1. Add the cauliflower florets to a big bowl.
2. In a small bowl, combine the olive oil with salt, garlic powder, Dijon mustard, and maple syrup. Brush the mixture over the florets and toss to coat.
3. Smoke the cauliflower until it is fork-tender and browned lightly. You will need to stir occasionally during smoking.
4. Garnish with fresh parsley and enjoy.

SMOKED JALAPENOS

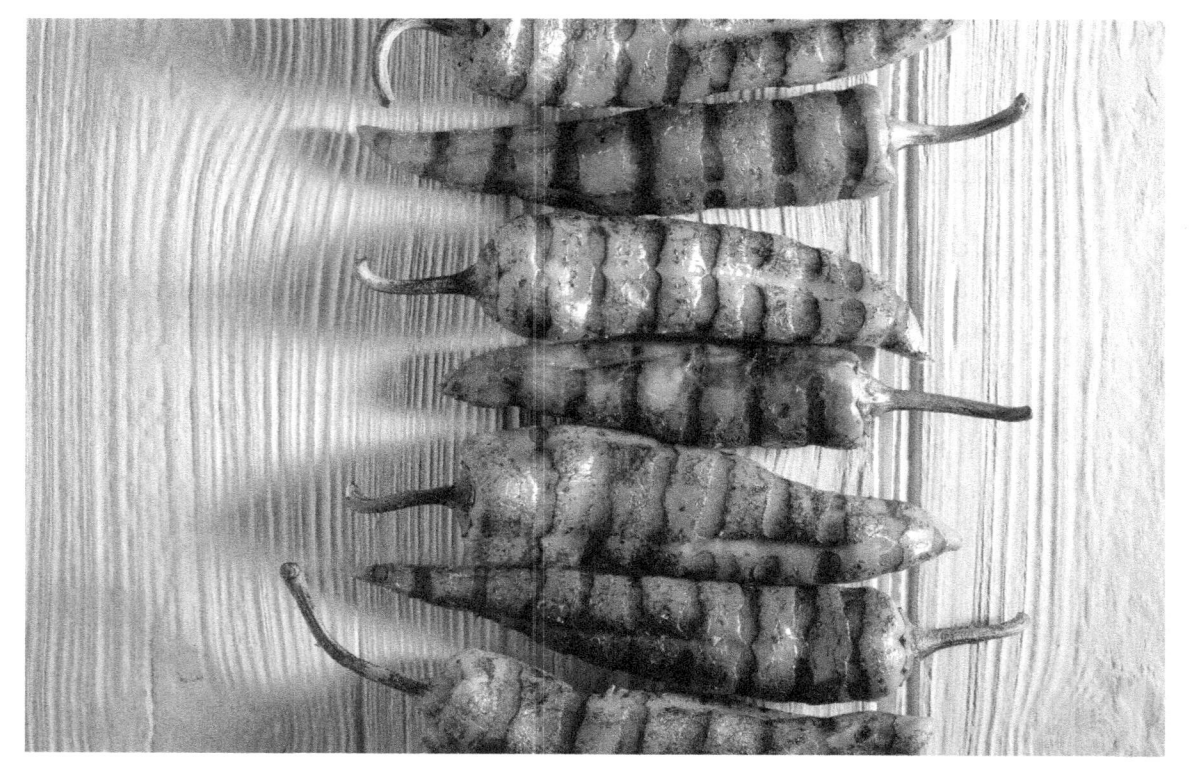

(TOTAL COOK TIME 4 HOURS 5 MINUTES)

INGREDIENTS FOR 15-20 SERVINGS

THE INGREDIENTS

- Large, ripe jalapenos (2-lb, 0.9-kg)

THE SMOKE

- Set the smoker to 250°F (120°C)
- Use pecan or apple wood chips for this recipe

METHOD

1. Place the jalapenos along with their stems, seeds and membranes rack in a single layer, a little apart on a smoker rack or tray. Close the lid and smoke the jalapenos. Place the peppers on the hotspot, as this will avoid you having to move them around.
2. Smoke for 4 hours, checking their progress every 60 minutes. They are ready when they are blackened and dark and appear leather-like.
3. Remove from the smoker and enjoy.

SMOKED NEW POTATO AND EGG SALAD

(TOTAL COOK TIME 11 HOURS)

INGREDIENTS FOR 8-10 SERVINGS

THE INGREDIENTS

- Baby new potatoes (2-lb, 0.9-kg)
- Olive oil – ⅓ cup
- Flakey sea salt – 1 teaspoon
- 6 hard-boiled eggs, cooled and peeled
- Onion, peeled and diced – ½ cup
- Celery, diced – ½ cup
- Cheddar cheese, shredded – 1½ cups
- Fresh chives, finely chopped – ¼ cup
- Thick-cut bacon, cooked and coarsely chopped (8-oz, 200-gm)

THE SAUCE

- Mayonnaise – 2 cups
- Dijon mustard – 2 tablespoons
- Sour cream – ½ cup
- Apple cider vinegar – 3 tablespoons
- Onion powder – ½ teaspoon
- Celery salt – ½ teaspoon

THE SMOKE

- Set the smoker to 220°F (105°C)

METHOD

1. Add the potatoes to a grill-safe roasting sheet.
2. Drizzle over the oil and shake the sheets to coat the potatoes evenly.
3. Season the potatoes with salt, and transfer to the smoker. Add the hard-boiled eggs and smoke for 30-45 minutes.
4. Smoke the potatoes for 2 hours while shaking and tossing the sheet for 25 minutes or so. Remove the potatoes from the smoker when they are easy to pierce when using a fork.
5. Slice the potatoes into ¼s or ½s to bite-size chunks.
6. Chop the eggs and add them to a bowl along with the sauce ingredients (mayonnaise, mustard, sour cream, apple cider vinegar, onion powder, and celery salt). Add the celery and onion to the mixture and mix to combine.
7. Add the cold potato chunks to the sauce and toss until evenly coated.
8. Transfer the potato salad to the fridge overnight.
9. When ready to serve, fold in the chopped bacon, Cheddar cheese, and chives.
10. Serve and enjoy.

BUTTER SMOKED CABBAGE

(TOTAL COOK TIME 6 HOURS 15 MINUTES)

INGREDIENTS FOR 4-6 SERVINGS

THE VEGETABLES

- 1 cabbage

THE INGREDIENTS

- Irish salted butter – ½ cup
- All-purpose rub – 2 tablespoons
- White balsamic vinegar – 2 tablespoons
- Freshly ground black pepper, to season

THE SMOKE

- Preheat the smoker to 250°F (120°C)

METHOD

1. First, core the cabbage and put 1 large size leaf to one side.
2. Rub the butter, in layers, inside the core until it is filled. Season all over with all-purpose rub. Using your finger, make a well shape inside the butter.
3. Pour the vinegar into the well to fill.
4. Place the large cabbage leaf over the top to secure.
5. Smoke for 4 hours before removing from the smoker, wrapping in aluminum foil, and continue to smoke for 2 hours, until your preferred level of tenderness.
6. Season with black pepper and serve.

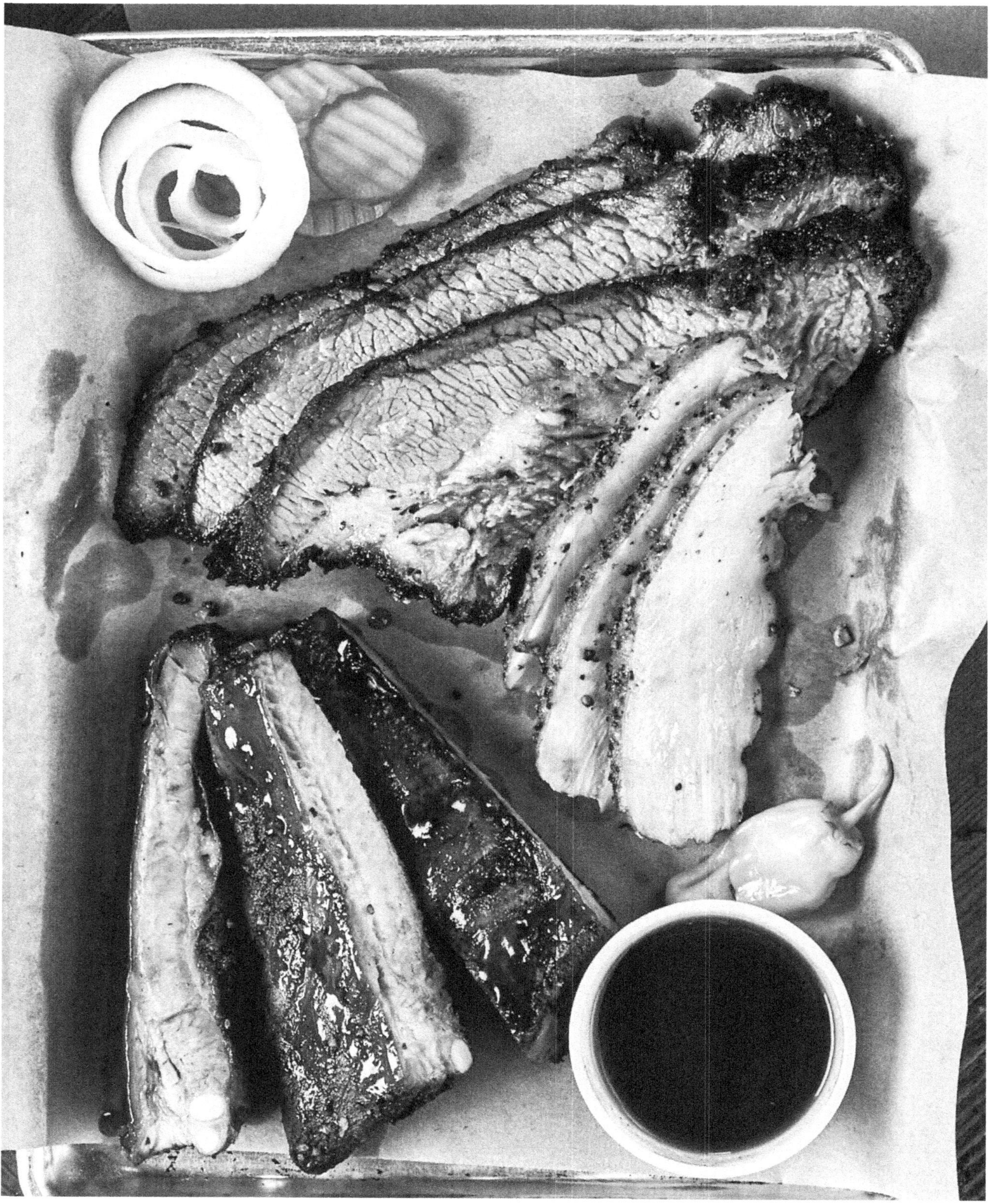

CHAPTER 10
SAUCES

CRANBERRY BBQ SAUCE - 184
ROASTED GARLIC PEPPERCORN SAUCE - 186
PLUM SOY GLAZE FOR HAM - 188
SWEET AND SPICY APRICOT BASTING SAUCE - 189
BUTTER BBQ SAUCE - 190
BRINE FOR SMOKED SALMON - 192
DUCK CURE - 194
ASIAN DRY RUB - 195

CRANBERRY BBQ SAUCE

(TOTAL COOK TIME 20 MINUTES)

INGREDIENTS FOR 3 CUPS

THE INGREDIENTS

- Canned whole-berry cranberry sauce – 1 ½ cups
- BBQ sauce, store-bought –1 ½ cups
- Ground cinnamon – 1 teaspoon
- Chili powder – 1 teaspoon
- Ground cumin – 1 teaspoon
- Black pepper – 1 teaspoon
- Salt – ½ teaspoon

METHOD

1. In a saucepan, combine the cranberry sauce, BBQ sauce, ground cinnamon, chili powder, ground cumin, black pepper, and salt. Heat the mixture through.
2. Set the sauce aside to cool completely.
3. Store the sauce in a resealable container in the fridge for up to 28 days.
4. To serve, reheat the sauce

ROASTED GARLIC PEPPERCORN SAUCE

(TOTAL TIME 1 HOUR 5 MINUTES)

INGREDIENTS FOR 2 CUPS

THE INGREDIENTS

- 1 whole head garlic, peeled
- Olive oil – 1 teaspoon
- Butter – 2 tablespoons
- All-purpose flour – 1½ tablespoons
- Milk – 1½ cups
- Salt – ½ teaspoon
- Ground mixed peppercorns – 1 tablespoon
- A pinch of ground nutmeg

METHOD

1. Preheat the main oven to 325°F (160°C).
2. Slice the top third of the garlic head off to expose the tips of the cloves. Transfer to a small baking dish and pour in just enough water to cover the bottom of the baking dish.
3. Drizzle the oil over the top of the garlic. Cover the dish with either a lid or aluminum foil. Roast the garlic in the oven for 45 minutes.
4. In a pan, over moderate heat, melt the butter.
5. Mix the flour with the milk until lump-free. Then pour it into the pan with the melted butter. Bring to a boil, and while constantly stirring, cook for around 5 minutes, until thickened.
6. Squeeze the garlic cloves out of their skin and mash.
7. Add the garlic to the sauce, and season with salt, mixed peppercorns, and ground nutmeg.
8. Serve.

PLUM SOY GLAZE FOR HAM

(TOTAL TIME 10 MINUTES)

INGREDIENTS FOR 2 ¼ CUPS

THE INGREDIENTS

- Plum jam – 1 cup
- Firmly packed brown sugar – ½ cup
- Cranberry juice – ½ cup
- Light soy sauce – ¼ cup

METHOD

1. Add the plum jam, brown sugar, cranberry juice, and light soy sauce to a pan and set over moderately high heat. Bring the glaze to a simmer, and cook, stirring until slightly thickened, for 5 minutes.
2. Use as needed.

SWEET AND SPICY APRICOT BASTING SAUCE

(TOTAL TIME 20 MINUTES)

INGREDIENTS FOR 2 CUPS

THE INGREDIENTS

- Apricot jam – 1 cup
- White vinegar – ½ cup
- Worcestershire sauce – 3 tablespoons
- Dijon mustard – 2 tablespoons
- Honey – 2 tablespoons
- Crushed red pepper – 2 teaspoons

METHOD

1. In a small pan, combine the apricot jam, white vinegar, Worcestershire sauce, Dijon mustard, honey, and red pepper. Heat over moderate heat until the jam and honey melt.
2. Brush the baste over the meat at the end of the grilling process.

BUTTER BBQ SAUCE

(TOTAL TIME 15 MINUTES)

INGREDIENTS FOR 2 CUPS

THE INGREDIENTS

- Butter – ½ cup
- Onion, peeled and chopped – ½ cup
- Catsup – ½ cup
- Worcestershire sauce – 3 tablespoons
- Firmly packed light brown sugar – ¼ cup
- Chili powder – 1½ teaspoons
- Salt – 1 teaspoon
- Black pepper - ⅛ teaspoon
- Tabasco sauce, as needed, to taste

METHOD

1. In a pan, melt the butter.
2. Add the onion to the melted butter, and cook until tender.
3. Add the catsup, Worcestershire sauce, brown sugar, chili powder, salt, black pepper, and Tabasco sauce, to taste. Stir the sauce to combine and simmer for approximately 5 minutes.
4. Serve.

BRINE FOR SMOKED SALMON

(TOTAL TIME 10 MINUTES)

INGREDIENTS FOR 20+ CUPS

THE INGREDIENTS

- Water – 16 cups
- Kosher salt – 1 cup
- White sugar – 1 cup
- Brown sugar – 1 cup
- Lemon pepper, to season
- 1 package dry seafood seasoning mix (3-oz, 85-gm)
- Freshly ground black pepper to season
- 4 garlic cloves, peeled and crushed
- A dash of hot pepper sauce to season
- 4 fresh lemons, peeled, sliced, seeded, and crushed
- 2 fresh oranges, peeled, seeded, sliced, and crushed
- 1 fresh lime, peeled, seeded, sliced, and crushed
- 1 large onion, peeled and sliced

METHOD

1. Pour the water into a small bucket. Add the kosher salt, white and brown sugars, lemon pepper, seafood seasoning, and black pepper. Then, add the garlic, hot pepper sauce, crushed lemon, crushed orange, crushed lime, and onion.
2. To use, soak the salmon in the brine in the fridge for 12-36 hours. Then, smoke the salmon as directed.

DUCK CURE

(TOTAL TIME 15 MINUTES)

INGREDIENTS FOR 1¼ CUPS

THE INGREDIENTS

- Brown sugar (3.5-oz, 100-gm)
- Coarse salt (4.6-oz, 130-gm)
- Sichuan peppercorns, crushed – 2 teaspoons
- Fennel seeds, crushed – 1 teaspoon

METHOD

1. Combine the brown sugar, coarse salt, Sichuan peppercorns, and fennel seeds in a bowl.
2. To use, spread around ⅓ of the cure in the bottom of a dish that is a snug fit for the duck. Place the duck fillet skin side facing up and completely cover the remaining cure. Cover with kitchen wrap and transfer to the fridge for 72 hours.
3. Use as directed in your recipe.

ASIAN DRY RUB

(TOTAL TIME 5 MINUTES)

INGREDIENTS FOR ⅓ CUP

THE INGREDIENTS

- Dried basil – 4 teaspoons
- Dried mint – 4 teaspoons
- Salt – 2 teaspoons
- Ground ginger – 2 teaspoons
- Paprika – 2 teaspoons
- Ground red pepper – 1½ teaspoons
- Freshly ground black pepper – 1 teaspoon
- Garlic powder – ½ teaspoon

METHOD

1. In a Mason jar, combine all the ingredients (dried basil, dried mint, salt, ground ginger, paprika, red pepper, black pepper, and garlic powder).
2. Seal the jar with its lid, and store for up to 14 days.
3. Use as needed.

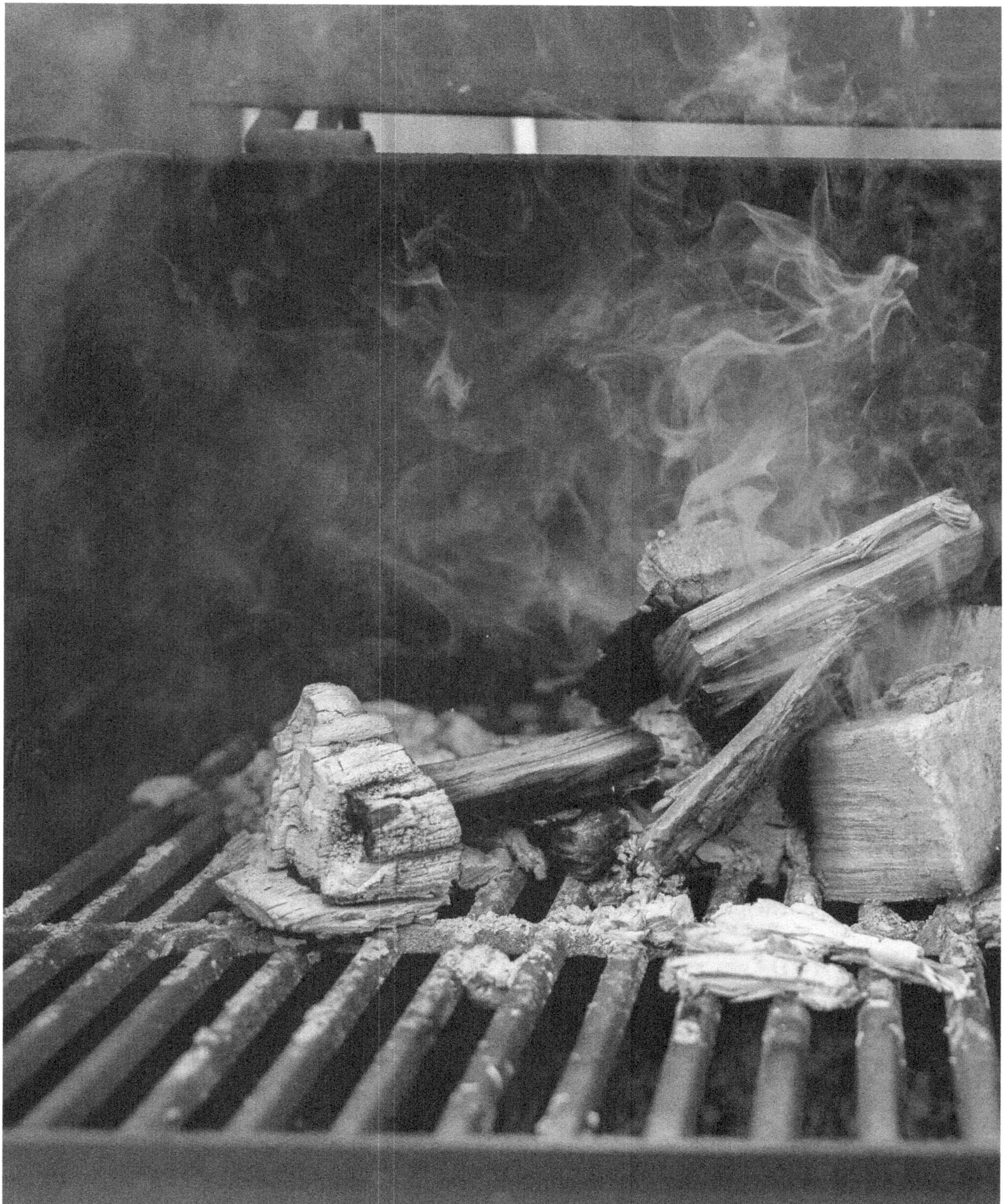

CHAPTER 11
SMOKING MEAT BASIC

BARBECUING AND SMOKING MEAT - 198
COLD AND HOT SMOKING - 199
SELECTING A SMOKER - 200
DIFFERENT SMOKER TYPES - 201
DIFFERENT SMOKER STYLES - 202
CHOOSE YOUR WOOD - 203
CHARCOAL - 205
RIGHT TEMPERATURE - 206
BASIC PREPARATIONS - 207
ELEMENTS OF SMOKING - 208

BARBECUING AND SMOKING MEAT

You might not believe it, but there are still people who think that the process of Barbequing and Smoking are the same! So, this is something you should know about before diving deeper. So, whenever you use a traditional BBQ grill, you always put your meat directly on top of the heat source for a brief amount of time which eventually cooks up the meal. Smoking, on the other hand, will require you to combine the heat from your grill as well as the smoke to infuse a delicious smoky texture and flavor into your meat. As a result, smoking usually takes much longer than traditional barbecuing. In most cases, it takes a minimum of 2 hours and a temperature of 100 -120 degrees for the smoke to be properly infused into the meat. Keep in mind that the time and temperature will depend on the type of meat you are using, which is why it is suggested to keep a meat thermometer handy to ensure that your meat is doing fine. Also, remember that this barbecuing method is also known as "Low and slow" smoking. With that cleared up, you should be aware that there are two different ways smoking is done.

COLD AND HOT SMOKING

Depending on the type of grill that you are using, you can get the option to go for a Hot Smoking Method or a Cold Smoking One. However, the primary fact about these three different cooking techniques which you should keep in mind are as follows:

- **HOT SMOKING**: In this technique, the food will use both the heat on your grill and the smoke to prepare your food. This method is most suitable for chicken, lamb, brisket, etc.
- **COLD SMOKING:** In this method, you are going to smoke your meat at a very low temperature, such as 85 F (30 degrees Celsius), making sure that it doesn't come into direct contact with the heat. Cold smoking is mainly used
- **ROASTING SMOKE:** This is also known as Smoke Baking. This process is essentially a combined form of roasting and baking and can be performed in any smoker with a capacity to reach temperatures above 180 F (80 degrees Celsius).

SELECTING A SMOKER

You need to invest in a good smoker if you smoke meat regularly. Consider these options when buying a smoker. Here are two natural fire options for you:

- **CHARCOAL SMOKERS**: are fueled by a combination of charcoal and wood. Charcoal burns quickly, and the temperature remains steady so you won't have any problem with a charcoal smoker. The wood gives a great flavor to the meat, and you will enjoy smoking meat.
- **WOOD SMOKER:** The wood smoker will give your brisket and ribs the best smoky flavor and taste, but it is harder to cook with wood. Both hardwood blocks and chips are used as fuel.

DIFFERENT SMOKER TYPES

You should know that in the market, you will get three different types of Smokers

CHARCOAL SMOKER

These smokers are hands down the best for infusing the perfect smoky flavor to your meat. But be warned that these smokers are difficult to master as the method of regulating temperature is a little bit difficult compared to standard Gas or Electric smokers.

ELECTRIC SMOKER

After the charcoal smoker, next comes the more straightforward option, Electric Smokers. These are easy-to-use and plug-and-play types. All you need to do is plug in, set the temperature, and go about your daily life. The smoker will do the rest. However, remember that the smoky finishing flavor won't be as intense as the Charcoal one.

GAS SMOKERS

Finally, comes the Gas Smokers. These have a reasonably easy temperature control mechanism and are usually powered by LP Gas. The drawback of these Smokers is that you will have to keep checking up on your smoker now and then to ensure that it has enough Gas.

DIFFERENT SMOKER STYLES

The different styles of Smokers are essentially divided into the following.

VERTICAL (BULLET STYLE USING CHARCOAL)

These are usually low-cost solutions and are perfect for first-time smokers.

VERTICAL (CABINET STYLE)

These Smokers have a square-shaped design with cabinets and drawers/trays for easy accessibility. These cookers come with a water tray and a designated wood chips box.

OFFSET

These types of smokers have dedicated fireboxes that are attached to the side of the main grill. The smoke and heat required for these are generated from the firebox, which is passed through the main chamber and out through a nicely placed chimney.

KAMADO JOE

And finally, we have the Kamado Joe, which ceramic smokers are largely regarded as being the "Jack of All Trades."

These smokers can be used as low and slow smokers, grills, high or low-temperature ovens, and so on.

They have a thick ceramic wall that allows them to hold heat better than any other smoker, requiring only a little charcoal.

These are easy to use with better insulation and are more efficient when it comes to fuel control.
comes to fuel control.

CHOOSE YOUR WOOD

You need to choose your wood carefully because the type of wood you will use affect significantly to the flavor and taste of the meat. Here are a few options for you:

- **MAPLE**: Maple has a smoky and sweet taste and goes well with pork or poultry
- **ALDER**: Alder is sweet and light. Perfect for poultry and fish.
- **APPLE**: Apple has a mild and sweet flavor. Goes well with pork, fish, and poultry.
- **OAK**: Oak is great for slow cooking. Ideal for game, pork, beef, and lamb.
- **MESQUITE**: Mesquite has a smoky flavor and is extremely strong. Goes well with pork or beef.
- **HICKORY**: Has a smoky and strong flavor. Goes well with beef and lamb.
- **CHERRY**: Has a mild and sweet flavor. Great for pork, beef, and turkey

The Different Types Of Wood	Suitable For
Hickory	Wild game, chicken, pork, cheeses, beef
Pecan	Chicken, pork, lamb, cheeses, fish.
Mesquite	Beef and vegetables
Alder	Swordfish, Salmon, Sturgeon and other types of fishes. Works well with pork and chicken too.
Oak	Beef or briskets
Maple	Vegetable, ham or poultry
Cherry	Game birds, poultry or pork
Apple	Game birds, poultry, beef
Peach	Game birds, poultry or pork
Grape Vines	Beef, chicken or turkey
Wine Barrel Chips	Turkey, beef, chicken or cheeses
Seaweed	Lobster, mussels, crab, shrimp etc.
Herbs or Spices such as rosemary, bay leaves, mint, lemon peels, whole nutmeg etc.	Good for cheeses or vegetables and a small collection of light meats such as fillets or fish steaks.

CHARCOAL

In General, there are three different types of charcoal. All of them are porous residues of black color made of carbon and ashes. However, the following are a little distinguishable due to their specific features.

- **BBQ BRIQUETTES:** These are the ones that are made from a fine blend of charcoal and char.

- **CHARCOAL BRIQUETTES:** These are created by compressing charcoal and are made from sawdust or wood products.

- **LUMP CHARCOAL**: These are made directly from hardwood and are the most premium quality charcoals. They are entirely natural and are free from any form of additives.

RIGHT TEMPERATURE

- Start at 250F (120C): Start your smoker a bit hot. This extra heat gets the smoking process going.

- Temperature drop: Once you add the meat to the smoker, the temperature will drop, which is fine.

- Maintain the temperature. Monitor and maintain the temperature. Keep the temperature steady during the smoking process.

Avoid peeking now and then. Smoke and heat are the two crucial elements that make your meat taste great. If you open the cover every now, and then you lose both of them, and your meat loses flavor. Only open the lid only when you truly need it.

BASIC PREPARATIONS

- Always be prepared to spend the whole day and take as much time as possible to smoke your meat for maximum effect.
- Ensure you obtain the perfect Ribs/Meat for the meal you are trying to smoke. Do a little bit of research if you need.
- I have already added a list of woods. Consult that list and choose the perfect wood for your meal.
- Make sure to prepare the marinade for each of the meals properly. A great deal of the flavors comes from the rubbing.
- Keep a meat thermometer handy to get the internal temperature when needed.
- Use mittens or tongs to keep yourself safe.
- Please refrain from using charcoal infused alongside starter fluid, as it might bring a very unpleasant odor to your food.
- Always start with a small amount of wood and keep adding them as you cook.
- Don't be afraid to experiment with different types of wood for newer flavors and experiences.
- Always keep a notebook near you and note jot down whatever you are doing or learning and use them during future sessions. A notebook will help you to evolve and move forward.

ELEMENTS OF SMOKING

Smoking is a very indirect method of cooking that relies on many factors to give you the most perfectly cooked meal you are looking for. Each component is essential to the whole process as they all work together to create the meal of your dreams.

- **TIME**: Unlike grilling or even Barbequing, smoking takes a long time and requires a lot of patience. It takes time for the smoky flavor to get infused into the meats slowly. Just to compare things, it takes about 8 minutes to thoroughly cook a steak through direct heating, while smoking (indirect heating) will take around 35-40 minutes.
- **TEMPERATURE:** When it comes to smoking, the temperature is affected by many factors that are not only limited to the wind and cold air temperatures but also the cooking wood's dryness. Some smokers work best with large fires that are controlled by the draw of a chimney and restricted airflow through the various vents of the cooking chamber and firebox. At the same time, other smokers tend to require minor fire with fewer coals and a completely different combination of the vent and draw controls. However, most smokers are designed to work at temperatures as low as 180 degrees Fahrenheit to as high as 300 degrees Fahrenheit. But the recommended temperature usually falls between 250 degrees Fahrenheit and 275 degrees Fahrenheit.
- **AIRFLOW**: The air to which the fire is significantly exposed determines how your fire will burn and how quickly it will burn the fuel. For instance, if you restrict airflow into the firebox by closing up the available vents, the fire will burn at a low temperature and vice versa. Typically in smokers, after lighting up the fire, the vents are opened to allow for maximum airflow and are then adjusted throughout the cooking process to ensure that optimum flame is achieved.
- **INSULATION:** Insulation is also essential for smokers as it helps to manage the cooking process throughout the whole cooking session. Good insulation allows smokers to reach the desired temperature instead of waiting hours!

CHAPTER 12
SAFETY

CLEANLINESS OF THE MEAT - 210
KEEPING YOUR MEAT COLD - 212
KEEPING YOUR MEAT COVERED - 212
PREVENTING FORMS OF CROSS-CONTAMINATION - 213
KNIVES - 213

CLEANLINESS OF THE MEAT

If you can follow the steps below, you will be able to ensure that your meat is safe from any bacterial or airborne contamination.

This first step is essential as no market-bought or freshly cut meat is entirely sterile.

Following these would significantly minimize the risk of getting affected by diseases.

- Make sure to properly wash your hands before beginning to process your meat. Use fresh tap water and soap/hand sanitizer.
- Make sure to remove metal ornaments such as rings and watches from your wrist and hand before handling the meat.
- Thoroughly clean the cutting surface using sanitizing liquid to remove any grease or unwanted contaminants. If you want a homemade sanitizer, you can simply make a solution of 1 part chlorine bleach and ten parts water.
- The sanitizer mentioned above should also be used to soak your tools, such as knives and other equipment, to ensure that they are safe to use.
- Alternatively, commercial acid based/ no rinsed sanitizers such as Star San will also work.
- After each use, all knives and other equipment, such as meat grinders, slicers, extruders, etc., should be cleaned thoroughly using soap water. The knives should be taken care in particular by cleaning the place just on top of the handle as it might contain blood and pieces of meat.
- When cleaning the surface, you should use cloths or sponges.

A note of sponges/clothes: It is ideal that you keep your sponge or cleaning cloth clean as it might result in cross-contamination. These are ideal harboring places for foodborne pathogens. Just follow the simple steps to ensure that you are on the safe side:
- Make sure to clean your sponge daily. It is seen that the effectiveness of cleaning it increases if you microwave the dam sponge for 1 minute and disinfect it using a solution of ¼ -1/2 teaspoon of concentrated bleach. This process will kill 99% of bacteria.
- Replace your sponge frequently, as using the same sponge every time (even with wash) will result in eventual bacterial growth.
- When not using the sponge, please keep it dry and wring it off of any loose food or debris.

KEEPING YOUR MEAT COLD

Mismanagement of temperature is one of the most common reasons for outbreaks of foodborne diseases. The study has shown that bacteria grow best at temperatures of 40 to 140 degree Fahrenheit/4-60 degree Celsius, which means that if not taken care of properly, bacteria in the meat will start to multiply very quickly. The best way to prevent this is to keep your meat cold before using it. Keep them eat in your fridge before processing them and make sure that the temperature is below 40 degrees Fahrenheit/4 degree Celsius.

KEEPING YOUR MEAT COVERED

All foods start to diminish once they are opened from their packaging or exposed to the air. However, the effect can be greatly minimized if you cover or wrap the foods properly.
The same goes for meat.
Good ways of keeping your meat covered and wrapped include:
- Using aluminum foil to cover up your meat will help to protect it from light and oxygen and keep the moisture intact. However, since Aluminum is reactive, it is advised that a layer of plastic wrap is used underneath the aluminum foil to provide a double protective coating.
- If the meat is kept in a bowl with no lid, then plastic wrap can seal the bowl, providing an airtight enclosure.
- Re-sealable bags protect by storing them in a bag and squeezing out any air.
- Airtight glass or plastic containers with lids are good options as well.
- A type of paper known as Freezer paper is specifically designed to wrap foods to be kept in the fridge. These wraps are excellent for meat as well.
- Vacuum sealers are often used for Sous Vide packaging. These machines are a bit expensive but can provide excellent packaging by completely sucking out any air from a re-sealable bag. This greatly increases the meat's shelf life outside and in the fridge.

PREVENTING FORMS OF CROSS-CONTAMINATION

Cross-Contamination usually occurs when one food comes into contact with another. In our case, we are talking about our meats.

This can be avoided very easily by keeping the following things in check:

- Always wash your hands thoroughly with warm water. The cutting boards, counters, knives, and other utensils should also be cleaned as instructed in the chapter's first section.
- Keep different types of meat in separate bowls, dishes, and plates before using them.
- When storing the meat in the fridge, keep the raw meat, seafood, poultry, and eggs on the bottom shelf of your fridge and in individual sealed containers.
- Keep your refrigerator shelves cleaned, and juices from meat/vegetables might drip on them.
- Always refrain from keeping raw meat/vegetables on the same plate as cooked goods.
- Always clean your cutting boards and use different cutting boards for different foods. Raw meats, vegetables, and other foods should be cut using a different table.

KNIVES

KNIVES: Sharp knives should be used to slice the meat accordingly. While using the knife, you should keep the following in mind.

- Always make sure to use a sharp knife
- Never hold a knife under your arm or leave it under a piece of meat
- Always keep your knives within visible distance
- Always keep your knife point down
- Always cut down towards the cutting surface and away from your body
- Never allow children to toy with knives unattended
- Wash the knives while cutting different types of food

CONCLUSION

I am happy to share this cookbook with you, and I take pride in offering you an extensive array of recipes that you will love and enjoy. I hope you benefit from each of our recipes, and I am sure you will like all the recipes we have offered you. Don't hesitate to try our creative and easy-to-make recipes, and remember that I have put my heart into coming up with delicious meals for you. If you like my recipes, you can share them with acquaintances and friends. I need your encouragement to continue writing more books!

P.S. Thank you for reading this book. If you've enjoyed this book, please don't shy; drop me a line, leave feedback, or both on Amazon. I love reading feedback and your opinion is extremely important to me.

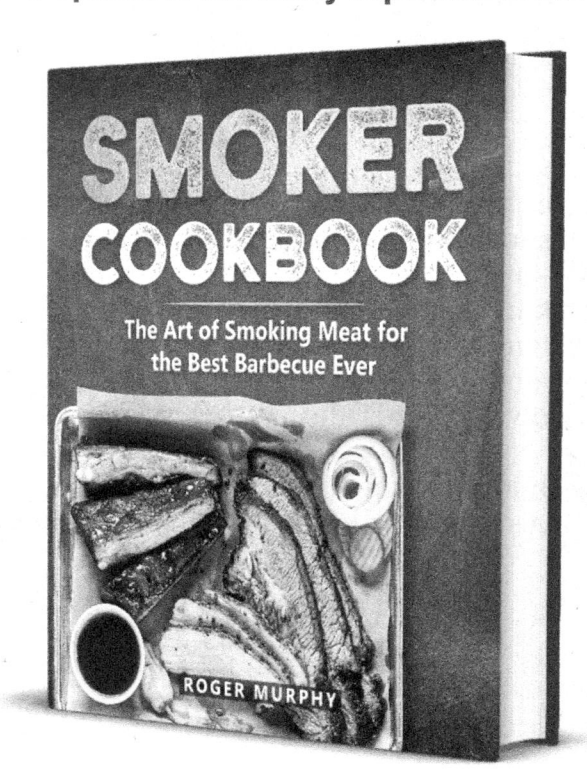

Copyright 2022© Roger Murphy

All rights reserved. No part of this guide may be reproduced in any form without permission in writing from the publisher except in the case of brief quotations embodied in critical articles or reviews.

Legal & Disclaimer: The information contained in this book and its contents is not designed to replace or take the place of any form of medical or professional advice; and is not meant to replace the need for independent medical, financial, legal, or other professional advice or services, as may be required. The content and information in this book have been provided for educational and entertainment purposes only. The content and information in this book have been compiled from reliable sources, and it is accurate to the best of the Author's knowledge, information, and belief. However, the Author cannot guarantee its accuracy and validity and cannot be held liable for errors and omissions. Further, changes are periodically made to this book as and when needed. Therefore, where appropriate and necessary, you must consult a professional (including but not limited to your doctor, attorney, financial advisor, or such other professional advisor) before using any of the suggested remedies, techniques, or information in this book.

Upon using the contents and information in this book, you agree to hold harmless the Author from and against any damages, costs, and expenses, including any legal fees potentially resulting from the application of any of the information provided.

This disclaimer applies to any loss, damages, or injury caused by the use and application, whether directly or indirectly, of any advice or information presented, whether for breach of contract, tort, negligence, personal injury, criminal intent, or under any other cause of action.

You agree to accept all risks of using the information presented in this book.

You agree that by continuing to read this book, where appropriate and necessary, you shall consult a professional (including but not limited to your doctor, attorney, financial advisor, or such other advisor as needed) before using any of the suggested remedies, techniques, or information in this book.

Made in the USA
Columbia, SC
20 December 2024